Jungian Theory for St<

Jungian Theory for Storytellers is a toolkit for anyone using Jungian archetypes to create stories in fiction, TV, film, video games, documentaries, poetry, and many other media. It contains a detailed classification of the archetypes, with relevant examples, and explains how they work in different types of narratives. Importantly, Bassil-Morozow explores archetypes and their significance in characterization, individuation, plot and story-building.

Bassil-Morozow also presents an overview of Jung's thoughts on creativity and other Jungian concepts, including the unconscious, ego, persona and self and the individuation process, and shows how they are linked to conflict. The book provides an explanation of relevant Jungian terms for a non-Jungian audience and introduces the idea of the hero's journey, with examples included throughout.

Accessibly written yet academic, both practical and engaging, and written with a non-Jungian audience in mind, *Jungian Theory for Storytellers* is an ideal source for writers and screenwriters of all backgrounds, including academics and teachers, who want to use Jungian theory in their work or are seeking to understand relevant Jungian ideas.

Helena Bassil-Morozow, PhD, is a cultural philosopher, media and film scholar, and academic writer whose many publications include *Tim Burton: The Monster and the Crowd*, *The Trickster in Contemporary Film* and *The Trickster and the System: Identity and Agency in Contemporary Society* (all Routledge). She is currently working on several other Routledge projects. She is a Lecturer in Media and Communication at Glasgow Caledonian University, UK. www.hbassilmorozow.com

Routledge Focus on Analytical Psychology

The Routledge Focus on Analytical Psychology series features short books covering unique, distinctive and cutting-edge topics. For a full list of titles in this series, please visit: https://www.routledge.com/Routledge-Focus-on-Analytical-Psychology/book-series/FOAP

Titles in the series:

Jungian Theory for Storytellers
A Toolkit

Helena Bassil-Morozow

Routledge
Taylor & Francis Group

LONDON AND NEW YORK

First published 2018
by Routledge

2 Park Square, Milton Park, Abingdon, Oxfordshire OX14 4RN
52 Vanderbilt Avenue, New York, NY 10017

*Routledge is an imprint of the Taylor & Francis Group, an informa
business*

First issued in paperback 2020

British Library Cataloguing in Publication Data
A catalogue record for this book is available from the British Library

Library of Congress Cataloging in Publication Data
A catalog record has been requested for this book

ISBN: 978-0-8153-5619-6 (hbk)
ISBN: 978-0-367-60706-7 (pbk)

Typeset in Times New Roman
by Swales & Willis Ltd, Exeter, Devon, UK

FOR KASPARS, MY MUSE

Contents

Acknowledgements

Firstly, I greatly appreciate the help and support offered to me by Kate Hawes and Susannah Frearson at Routledge.

I would also like to thank my department at Glasgow Caledonian University, and particularly Christina McIntyre, for her continuing support and guidance. Christina's invaluable advice and comments made this book more accessible and – I am pretty sure – more engaging!

A big *Thank You* to Katya Bystreetsky whose beautiful illustrations adorn this book.

Finally, I would like to thank Kaspars for being an understanding and patient partner of a workaholic academic.

Introduction
How to use the toolkit

This book is for those who want to learn more about archetypes and the individuation process from the point of view of someone who creates or critiques stories. It is fairly general, accessibly written, and not limited to one storytelling format or genre, making it suitable for screenwriters, fiction authors, video game creators, and many more.

It offers a detailed description, with examples, of the building blocks of storytelling from the Jungian point of view, including nine archetypes and the individuation process. Chapter 2 contains an overview of archetypes in general, while Chapter 3 contains a taxonomy of archetypes in relation to storytelling as well as a comprehensive classification of the three major themes to which they belong in narratives. These are stand-alone chapters and can be used separately if you only want to know how to sketch a journey of self-discovery using archetypes. Additionally, the book gives an overview of other major Jungian ideas, and links them to the creative process: the collective and personal unconscious, the ego, the persona and the self, and Jung's views on creativity. If you want to see the bigger picture or want an introduction to Jungian psychology beyond his most popular ideas, read the whole book.

My task in this book was not to create a perfect, all-encompassing system which would describe every possible character or combination of characters out there. Examples given in the text and the taxonomy are also not comprehensive, and many of you can come up with your own examples.

Another thing I would like to remove from the toolkit is fixed-order sequences. Classical Jungian theory sees the individuation process as a fixed sequence, starting with the encounter with the shadow, moving to the anima or animus, then to the old wise man or woman, and so on. His disciple Jolande Jacobi outlined this sequence in her book *The Psychology of C. G Jung* (1942). Joseph Campbell in *The Hero with a Thousand Faces* (1949), and later Christopher Vogler in *The Writer's Journey: Mythic Structure for Writers* (1992) came up with their own sequences for the hero's journey. My argument, however, is that narratives do not have a 'fixed' order in which things happen to characters. This became clear with the advent of VOD television, when Hollywood's preferred standard two-hour 'hero myth' became challenged by longer formats with more complex hierarchies of meaning and richer archetypal arrangements. There are narratives dominated by one archetype, or two archetypes, and there are whole hierarchies of images none of whom is a hero on a Campbell-style journey. My advice, therefore, would be to see the taxonomy as a flexible toolkit which you can use to create your own combinations of images and meanings. Look at it as a box of possible characters – just take what you need out of it. The only distinction I would like to make here is that between the protagonist and other characters.

Finally, I would like to note that the taxonomy is a skeleton, and does not in itself contain deep meanings or interpretations. It is not linked to any specific medium, style or genre, or social content. All the complexity of interpretations in a narrative come with the complexity of characters and relationships; they are also fleshed out in linguistic, stylistic, socio-political, genre differences. One can analyse and interpret acting, costumes, dialogues and descriptions, camera angles, editing choices and other textual divisions, choice of filter, use of sound within a narrative, tropes – but not the basic narrative structure because all meaning is contextual. The archetypal toolkit is essentially pre-meaning, but it allows authors to determine the direction and form their meanings will take, and where their meanings will flow at a later stage, when the skeleton has been hidden under contextualized information such as time, place, gender of the protagonist, and so on.

For references to the works of C. G. Jung: except where a different publication was used, all references are to the hardback edition of C. G. Jung, *The Collected Works* (CW), edited by Sir Herbert Read, Dr. Michael Fordham and Dr. Gerhardt Adler, and translated by R. F. C. Hull.

1   The unconscious
The birthplace of creativity

According to Jung, the creative process is born in the unconscious. In terms of narratives, the unconscious is also the moving force behind our characters' motivation, sense of direction, impulses, and both positive and negative emotions. The Jungian unconscious is, however, complex, and these motivations can come from one of two chambers: the collective, in which contents shared by all humankind, past and present, reside; or the personal, which is home to our unique issues and experiences.

The presence of the common psychological base – the collective unconscious – is important as it emphasizes the structural similarities of human narratives instead of concentrating on the cultural and personal differences. The collective unconscious consists of *archetypes* (discussed in detail in Chapter 2), whereas the personal unconscious is home to individual contents such as memories, fantasies and complexes (examined later in this chapter).

The collective unconscious

Jung defines the collective unconscious as a system that exists independently from the individual, has nothing to do with personal experience, and contains universal characters and behaviour patterns we all know and recognize (parental figures, romantic partner; growing up, falling in love, dealing with midlife crises, etc.). The collective unconscious is inherited, Jung argues (CW 9/I: para. 90).

It is thus an objective system, unknowable in its vastness. It is so much larger than individual consciousness that it is important to know yourself well in order to avoid being engulfed by it. Its influence, the effect of 'a merging of minds' and 'being at one with the world', is exciting and addictive. Human consciousness, Jung keeps reminding his readers, is but a tiny island in the ocean that is the collective unconscious:

the collective unconscious is anything but an encapsulated personal system; it is sheer objectivity, as wide as the world and open to all the world. There I am the object of every subject, in complete reversal of my ordinary consciousness, where I am always the subject that has an object. There I am utterly one with the world; so much a part of it that I forget all too easily who I really am. 'Lost in oneself' is a good way of describing this state. But this self is the world, if only a consciousness could see it. That is why we must know who we are.

(CW 9/I: 46)

Naturally, Jung realizes that a giant, objective (as he calls it) superstructure that has a 'mind' of its own and that is invisible to the human eye is a difficult and complex concept. Not all of his readers would be convinced. Some will start asking questions similar to the ones atheists ask believers: 'How do you know it exists if you cannot see it?' Jung attempts to forestall accusations of being unscientific by trying to give his concept a 'biological' base. The unconscious, he says, is not a mystical concept; far from it:

The hypothesis of the collective unconscious is, therefore, no more daring than to assume there are instincts. One admits readily that human activity is influenced to a high degree by instincts, quite apart from the rational motivations of the conscious mind. So if the assertion is made that that our imagination, perception, and thinking are likewise influenced by inborn and universally present formal elements, it seems to me that a normally functioning intelligence can discover in this idea as much or as little mysticism as in the theory of instincts.

(CW 9/I: para. 92)

Jung also gives his readers what he calls 'empirical' (verifiable by observation) proofs of the existence of the collective unconscious. There are several such proofs. The first is dreams, in which archetypes appear to us involuntarily, which proves that they are products of nature (CW 9/I: para. 100).

Then there is 'active imagination': 'a sequence of fantasies produced by deliberate concentration' (CW 9/I: para. 101). Active imagination is a good way of making otherwise hidden and repressed fantasies conscious. Imagine that you saw a flock of brightly coloured hot air balloons high up in the sky. Suddenly you imagine yourself riding in one of these balloons, breathing in fresh air, feeling simultaneously excited and scared, looking at the little dots that are people, the moving dots that are cars, at the incredible puffed-up clouds above and the green and yellow patchwork of forests and farm fields below. Why are you having this fantasy? Is it because you are afraid of heights? Or perhaps you feel trapped in your job or relationship, and dream of escaping? Maybe you find everyday existence dull, and look to the skies for salvation from reality? Do you secretly dream of being 'above it all'? In any case, stay with it, and let images and sensations flow out freely. Observe them, take note of them. Don't force them out or stifle them in. Stay in the moment and enjoy the rare meeting of the unconscious with consciousness.

Active imagination is spontaneous creativity, but it can be managed and directed to produce a creative product. In several of his articles concerning the role of the collective unconscious in the creative process, Jung criticizes Freud and his disciples for looking for the artist's personal problems (and particularly sexual issues) in the work of art. He believes that a novel or a painting is not simply a dump heap of its creator's unsolved, 'dirty' problems such as a secret desire for the mother or the wish that the rival sibling might fall off the balcony, but a true expression of the force that is bigger than any personal problem: the collective unconscious. Its contents, archetypes, 'appear . . . in the shaped material of art as the regulative principles that shape it; that is to say, only by inferences drawn from the finished work can we reconstruct the age-old original of the primordial image' (CW 15: para. 94). The magical process of the birth of works of art out of raw creativity will be discussed in detail in Chapter 5.

Finally, there are more problematic 'proofs' of the existence of the collective unconscious, such as psychotic delusions, 'fantasies observed in trance-like states' and 'dreams of early childhood, from the third to the fifth year' (CW 9/I: para. 50). Yet, Jung takes these types of evidence very seriously because the information contained in them is not meaningless. They contain a grain of truth and therefore deserve to be treated with respect. In his autobiography *Memories, Dreams, Reflections*, he writes about a schizophrenic female patient who was convinced that she heard God's voice in her body. Instead of dismissing this claim as nonsensical, Jung decided to listen to the voice and even discovered that it made 'some very sensible remarks' (Jung, 1962: 148).

Earlier in the book, he also recalls the case of a young woman who became mentally ill as a result of sexual abuse in the hands of her schoolmate as well as her brother. The traumatized patient was convinced that she lived on the moon, and that her heroic task was to kill a vampire who kidnapped women and children. After stalking her prey for several nights, she finally came face to face with the vampire:

> Suddenly he stood before her. He had several pairs of wings. His face and entire figure were covered by them, so that she could see nothing but his feathers. Wonder-struck, she was seized by curiosity to find out what he really looked like. She approached, hand on the knife. Suddenly the wings opened and a man of unearthly beauty stood before her. He enclosed her in his winged arms with an iron grip, so that she

could no longer wield the knife. In any case she was so spellbound by the vampire's look that she would not have been capable of striking. He raised her from the platform and flew off with her.

(1962: 151)

Even though the young woman was severely mentally ill, there is nothing unusual in this fantasy given the girl's previous experiences with predatory males. Since the beginning of the nineteenth century when Romanticism made vampires into symbols of predatory behaviour, they have been associated with seduction and sexual aggression. One interpretation of the fantasy could be that the victim was trying to make sense of her terrifying experiences, and perhaps attempting to restore her trust in men. The dream could also be interpreted as a revenge fantasy in which the roles of the victim and the aggressor are reversed.

After she was discharged and took a job as a nurse in a sanatorium, she shot and lightly wounded an assistant doctor who, Jung writes euphemistically, 'made a somewhat rash approach to her' (1962: 152). Jung was also shocked to learn that she was carrying the gun with her at all times in case she had to defend herself against sexual advances. The young woman's perception of men as potentially dangerous was confirmed once more by the incident with the assistant doctor. In this light, the image of the vampire created by her unconscious to make sense of the situation, in metaphorical terms, is a lucid and understandable response of a victimized female to a shameful, scary and confusing situation.

The vampire fantasy goes beyond the experiences of the individual female in hostile circumstances (the personal unconscious), and potentially throws light on the position of women in patriarchal societies in general, or the role of women in social structures. Jung argues that psychosis contains 'the old human conflicts', and whereas patients may appear to be apathetic or irrational, 'there is more going on in their minds, and more that is meaningful, than there seems to be' (1962: 149).

Thus, the collective unconscious finds its expression in dreams, active imagination and psychotic fantasies, and exists independently from the individual. It creates a universal picture of psychic life and reflects common experiences shared by all humankind. It needs to be treated with respect, despite our habit of dismissing things that look irrational to us, or things that we cannot control.

The personal unconscious

Whereas the collective unconscious contains general and universal patterns, and is shared by everyone, its personal counterpart reflects the issues of particular individuals. It rests below the threshold of consciousness, and is fairly superficial. Each of us has our own version of the personal unconscious as a direct response to our unique life. Jung explains its existence by the fact that human consciousness cannot hold many things at once, and some inevitably end up being repressed, forgotten or subliminally perceived (CW 7: para. 205). Instead of forever disappearing, this content, which cannot be kept in the congested consciousness because of the lack of space, ends up in this depository of human experiences – the personal unconscious.

If the collective unconscious is home to the archetypes, which are shared by everyone, the personal unconscious contains personal issues such as memories or complexes, which are unique (Jacobi, 1942: 37). A complex is a constellation of sensitive issues in an individual, 'a centre of functional disturbance, which becomes virulent in certain external and internal situations, when it may totally upset the psychic balance and dominate the whole personality' (Jacobi, 1942: 36). Complexes vary from individual to individual: one person may viciously compete with their father; another is obsessed with submissive women he can control; someone else may feel like a superhero or a saviour; a fourth thinks she is Mother Teresa. Popular culture seems to like the narrative potential of complexes. Any of Marvel's characters (for instance, Spider-Man, Iron Man or Hulk) may be described as possessing (and being possessed by) a complex which prevents them from feeling normal: anger complex, invincibility complex, etc.

Our personal unconscious makes itself known when, for instance, we have a dream about our boss whom we hate; when we suddenly feel an urge to call our elderly parents just to make sure they are fine; or when we catch a peripheral glimpse of an attractive person on the underground, and surreptitiously look again. Although transparent and fairly superficial, these impulses nevertheless are not fully digested and accepted by consciousness.

In all three cases, we may not even realize what we are doing, or why we are doing it. The information accompanying these events may not be fully available to consciousness. This is because we are trying to protect ourselves from unpleasant thoughts or emotional disasters; or perhaps this particular impulse or feeling is on its way to reach the threshold of consciousness, but is not yet there. In contrast with Freud's famous view of subliminal contents as being caused by unpleasant and therefore repressed childhood experiences, Jung emphasizes that the hidden thoughts are not necessarily repressed thoughts – they may simply be not developed or ripe enough for us to understand, and are 'waiting' for the right moment to become visible:

> In Freud's view, as most people know, the contents of the unconscious are reducible to infantile tendencies which are repressed because of their incompatible character. Repression is a process that begins in early childhood under the moral influence of the environment and continues

throughout life. By means of analysis the repression is removed and the repressed wishes made conscious.

According to this theory, the unconscious contains only those parts of the personality which could just as well be conscious, and have been suppressed only through the process of education. Although from one point of view the infantile tendencies of the unconscious are the most conspicuous, it would nonetheless be a mistake to define or evaluate the unconscious entirely in those terms. The unconscious has still another side to it: it includes not only repressed contents, but all psychic material that lies below the threshold of consciousness. It is impossible to explain the subliminal nature of all this material on the principle of repression.

(CW 7: para. 202–3)

Instead, Jung argues, some materials, such as an uncomfortable hunch or a pleasant sensation about a particular situation, 'have not yet reached the threshold of consciousness' (CW 7: para. 204). In this way, Jung adds a holistic dimension to the relationship between consciousness and the personal unconscious. They are simply engaging in dynamics, in a conversation; they are constantly managing and exchanging ideas, thoughts, feelings, premonitions, sensations, memories and intuitions.

In this way, we may dislike our boss but cannot express this hostility openly for fear of confrontation and possible damage. We may even lie to ourselves that she is likeable and has a range of positive qualities which offset the negative ones. Alternatively, we may not be aware of our feelings, and once this information reaches consciousness, we may take action – raise a complaint, confront the boss, or even resign.

We also love our parents and are afraid that they may die suddenly from a heart attack; perhaps we even feel guilty for not visiting them as often as we should. Or maybe the fear has nothing to do with repressed guilt, and is simply a realistic assessment of the situation by our personal unconscious. After all, we have to be prepared for all eventualities.

Finally, flirting with strangers on public transport is never a good idea as they are not likely to respond to our advances. On the other hand, we may simply not be aware of the impulse. Contents do not have to be repressed in order to be unconscious. They may just be waiting for the right moment to engage in a conversation with consciousness.

Jung's Romantic vision of the psyche

Jung's vision of the unconscious can be seen as ecological as well as in tune with nineteenth-century Romanticism, a movement that warned the

Western world of the dangers of modernity and lamented the demise of nature and the ruination of beautiful rural landscapes caused by the Industrial Revolution. The Jungian philosopher Susan Rowland writes that 'Jung takes a Romantic sensibility into anxieties about modernity and popular culture' (Rowland, 2005: 12).

Very much like the Romantics, Jung warns his readers about the dangers of modernity and urges them not to place too much confidence in the power of civilization and rationality. Consciousness, Jung maintains throughout his writings, is too self-assured. It tends to overestimate its own ability to handle instincts, feelings, emotions and projections. This overconfidence leads to inability to handle unconscious contents (dreams, fears, visions) when they arrive. Very often, these contents are simply repressed instead of being made conscious because 'it suits our hypertrophied and hubristic modern consciousness not to be mindful of the dangerous autonomy of the unconscious and to treat it negatively as an absence of consciousness' (CW 11: para. 141). Here, once more, Jung identifies consciousness as the driver of modernity and warns against the possible consequences of over-reliance on the rational approach to internal and external worlds.

Yet, Jung does not just criticize consciousness for being too arrogant and modernity for being disrespectful towards mother nature. We need both, consciousness and the unconscious, to maintain the psychic balance. Without consciousness, 'things go less well' (CW 8: 695). Consciousness also makes us aware of the dangers of identification with other human beings – of mass projections when whole nations are swept by an ideology, or when 'the other' is made into a scapegoat and blamed for a particular nation's failures. Consciousness makes it possible to analyse our feelings and emotions, and to disentangle them from those expressed by the people in our immediate environment or in mass media. It protects us from becoming 'part of the herd, from submersion into a common unconsciousness' (CW 10: para. 150). Every step in the direction of consciousness (to which education and self-reflection contribute greatly) means 'tearing oneself loose from the maternal womb of unconsciousness in which the mass of men dwells' (CW 10: para. 150). This mass of men, and what it can do to individual autonomy, will be examined in detail in Chapter 3, on individuation.

The unconscious: Jung versus Freud

The theory of the common psychological base for all mankind sets Jung's map of the psyche apart from that of Freud and his followers. It also focuses attention on the autonomous character of the collective unconscious; on its independence from individual characteristics.

Freud's vision of the unconscious – as a collection of childhood issues and personal problems – makes it look problematic but controllable. Thus, all issues human beings attempt to repress and disguise, even from themselves, have a logical, if not always pleasant, explanation. A cave, or some other dark natural cavity, in a dream represents a vagina. It could mean that one is sexually repressed. Leonardo's childhood dream of a vulture coming to his cradle and inserting its tail into his mouth is unequivocally interpreted by Freud as symbolizing oral sex (Freud, 1910: 86). Thus, the unconscious and its manifestations are deciphered as if they were a code, interpreted literally. Although unsafe, the unconscious is still controllable and has to be approached in a systematic and rational manner.

Not so much with Jung, who viewed the unconscious (and particularly its collective counterpart) as something mysterious; as something unpredictable and inexplicable. Its contents – dreams, fantasies, mental and emotional states, creative products – are seen as having autonomous existence, and rightfully so. They have to be treated with respect.

Jung called this respectful method of clarifying the (often obscure) material that comes out of the unconscious *amplification*, which involves offering and balancing multiple meanings of a dream or a fantasy in order to uncover 'a tissue of relationships in which the dream content is naturally embedded' (Jacobi, 1942: 77). For instance, equalling Leonardo's vulture dream with oral sex would be a very crude interpretation; not only because it involves rough imagery, but also because it is limited to sexuality and childhood complexes. In fact, Jung's student and colleague Erich Neumann produced an alternative interpretation of Leonardo's dream. For Neumann, even though Freud's explanation makes sense and is partially correct, it is still too narrow and does not take into account many other aspects of Leonardo's creative life:

Birds in general are symbols of the spirit and soul. [. . .]
    In connection with the infant lying in his cradle, the bird's tail is primarily a symbol of the maternal breast; but at the same time, Freud correctly interpreted it as the male genital organ. From this basic constellation emerging in the childhood memory, he attempted to derive both the personal mother complex of the fatherless Leonardo and a passively homosexual tendency in his love life. Both derivations are false and require a correction, since the 'vulture fantasy' is a transpersonal, archetypal constellation, and not one that may be derived personalistically from Leonardo's family romance.
    In the situation of the babe drinking at the maternal breast, the mother always represents the uroboric, i.e., male-female, greatness of the mother in relation to the child she bears, nourishes and protects. In this function, her life-giving breasts – as may be demonstrated in

primitive sculpture, for example – often become phallic symbols. In relation to which the child takes the attitude of receiving and conceiving. This is a fundamental human situation with nothing perverse or abnormal about it [. . .] The suprapersonal character of this experience for Leonardo is made clear by the fact that in his recollection the personal mother is meaningfully replaced by the bird symbol.

(Neumann, 1959: 8–9)

Neumann's treatment of the symbols in Leonardo's dream is more respectful than Freud's – both towards the artist and his creativity. He amplifies the imagery instead of sticking to a single definition. The tail is simultaneously a maternal breast, a male genital organ, a symbols of soul and spirit, the mother complex and an archetypal constellation representing the unconscious feeding the infant creativity. This is an exploration of Leonardo's situation rather than a definition. Neumann looks for symbolic, mythological and artistic parallels as well as biographical details. The multiple images result in a picture of baby Leonardo being fed by Mother Nature, emphasizing his special status as an individual with exceptional skills whose remarkable creativity flows straight out of the unconscious.

Everything below the conscious threshold also cannot be reduced to instinctual reactions and sexual drives. Years after his traumatic split from Freud, Jung kept arguing with his former master about the central role of the sexual instinct. The unconscious, Jung insists, is not pure biology: 'Anyone who penetrates into the unconscious with purely biological assumptions will become stuck in the instinctual sphere and unable to advance beyond it, for he will be pulled back again into physical existence' (CW 11: para. 843).

Criticizing Freud's approach to creative people, Jung writes that creativity, as a product of the unconscious, cannot be reduced to childhood complexes: 'Though the material he works with and its individual treatment can easily be traced back to the poet's personal relations with his parents, this does not enable us to understand his poetry' (CW 15: para. 99). He calls Freud's method reductive. To him, it is quite obviously an expression of consciousness' false belief in itself; a manifestation of its blunt, pseudo-scientific instrumentalism:

The essential thing in Freud's reductive method is to collect all the clues pointing to the unconscious background, and then, through the analysis and interpretation of this material, to reconstruct the elementary instinctual processes. [. . .] If we interpret Plato's metaphor [the Parable of the Cave] in Freudian terms we would naturally arrive at the uterus, and would have proved that even a mind like Plato's was still struck on a primitive level of infantile sexuality.

(CW 15: para. 105)

This kind of pseudo-scientism does not add much to the work of art. If anything, it makes it one-dimensional. A psychological factor, he writes, cannot be 'true' or 'correct', the existence of the factor is already a proof of its validity (CW 8: para. 192).

Note how Freud's vision of the unconscious is not only controllable and explainable, it is also mostly negative. There is little joy in its manifestations. It consists of symptoms which lead to the core problems, usually sexual and often originating in childhood. Freud's language – and the language of his colleagues – is awash with references to sexual organs: vagina, penis, breasts. All these range between literal and metaphorical meanings, and can be seen by individuals as 'good or bad'.

By contrast, Jung, who rejected the idea of sexuality as an issue that underlined most problems in life (and broke with Freud over this), sees the unconscious as a sort of cosmic ocean with a mind of its own. This mind is unknowable. It does not mean, however, that we cannot have a dialogue with it: we can. In fact, this vast cosmos wants to talk to us. It sends us cryptic signals, pictures and texts which we have to decipher. Our ability to guess what the unconscious has to say directly affects our path in life. This rather thoughtful and respectful attitude to the unconscious sets Jung apart from the Enlightenment tradition of Western thought. It also explains why, to this day, Jung's writings are seen as vague and his definitions unclear.

For over two centuries, the spirit of the Enlightenment has maintained that reason is here to control the creatures crawling out of the unconscious. By contrast, Jung maintains that the unconscious is a neutral rather than a monstrous phenomenon. He writes: 'The unconscious is not a demoniacal monster, but a natural entity which, as far as moral sense, aesthetic taste, and intellectual judgement go, is completely neutral. It only becomes dangerous when our conscious attitude to it is hopelessly wrong. To the degree that we repress it, the danger increases' (CW 16: para. 329).

Jung keeps emphasizing that human consciousness is not – as we Western people often think – the zenith of all creation. In this sense, his thinking is ecological. We are not the best in this universe. In fact, we should be grateful to nature for the fact of our existence, for the fact that we have been taken out of the dark depths of instinct: 'Our consciousness does not create itself – it wells up from unknown depths. In childhood it awakens gradually, and all through life it wakes up each morning out of the depths of sleep from an unconscious condition' (CW 11: para. 935).

People hoping to 'train' the unconscious to fit in with our vision of civilization and morality are destined to fail because it is 'an autonomous psychic entity', and any efforts to drill it will be simultaneously unsuccessful and harmful to consciousness (CW 12: para. 51). Importantly, we can plunge back into these depths at any time. Jung's reference to the consciousness waking up each morning is one of the many remarks warning human beings of the possible regression into madness. Conscious mind, Jung reminds us, is only the tip of the iceberg, and it is no match for the unconscious which, in spite all our efforts to re-associate repressed contents with consciousness, 'calmly goes on producing dreams and fantasies' (CW 7: para. 205).

Sometimes the unconscious can make one ill. In his autobiography *Memories, Dreams, Reflections*, co-written with his colleague Aniela Jaffé and published in 1962, Jung famously describes a series of terrible dreams he had in 1913 that prophesied the horrors of World War I. At the time, Jung was also going through a difficult time of separating from Freud and attempting to formulate his own ideas. The first of the dreams goes like this:

> In October [of 2013], while I was alone on a journey, I was suddenly seized by an overpowering vision: I saw a monstrous flood covering all the northern and low-lying lands between the North Sea and the Alps. When it came up to Switzerland I saw that the mountains grew higher and higher to protect our country. I realized that a frightful catastrophe was in progress. I saw mighty yellow waves, the floating rubble of civilization, and the drowned bodies of uncounted thousands. Then the whole sea turned to blood. This vision lasted about one hour. I was perplexed and nauseated, and ashamed of my weakness.
>
> (Jung, 1962: 199)

To Jung's despair, the vision returned two weeks later, 'even more vividly than before, and the blood was more emphasized. An inner voice spoke. "Look at it well, it is wholly real and it will be so. You cannot doubt it"' (1962: 199–200). The passage, with its mystic character, is quite in line with Jung's 'Romantic' vision of the unconscious. After all, World War I was the moment when the vision of modernity as a bringer of morality, rationality and the goodness of scientific progress was derailed. Suddenly, it became clear that human beings can be exceptionally cruel, and can use the fruits of technology and science to kill each other. The ideals of Enlightenment were thrown off their pedestals. Jung, who lived through both World War I and World War II, was particularly aware of the fragile barrier that separates civilized behaviour from barbaric aggression.

Further prophetic dreams and experiences of that period, which proved to be so turbulent for Jung, involved the land frozen to ice by an Arctic cold, then the cold arriving from the cosmos, the feeling of suddenly plunging into dark depths and discovering rivers of blood in the cave into which he fell, and an encounter with Biblical figures 'at the edge of a cosmic abyss' (1962: 203–5). These visions demonstrate well the kind of dialogue Jung envisaged with the unconscious. One does not just listen to the vision, however frightful. One also attempts to embrace it and looks forward to more messages as they arrive to offer clarification and guidance. The individual does not dominate the unconscious with his authority; rather, he lets it express itself and to produce images and messages, both pleasant and unpleasant. In other words, the individual, in the Jungian version, does not want to always be in control.

On the one hand, the voice was trying to guide Jung on his journey. On the other, it was showing him the journey of Europe. For Jung, the individual and the collective can never be completely separated. It was the collective unconscious which, Jung argues, exists in everyone and forms the underground base of our psyche that caused this simultaneous disturbance in his mental health and the mental health of the whole of Europe.

Jung admits later in the chapter that the disturbing visions and dreams he had in the years after his split with Freud laid the groundwork for his theory:

> Today I can say that I have never lost touch with my initial experiences. All my works, all my creative activity, has come from those initial fantasies and dreams which began in 1912, almost fifty years ago. Everything that I accomplished in later life was already contained in them, although at first only in the form of emotions and images.
>
> (1962: 217)

Moreover, Jung treated each of these experiences as a treasure and took great care to understand it, lest it 'strangled him like jungle creepers' (1962: 218). Rather like an astrophysicist studying heavenly bodies, their messages and the superstructure uniting them, Jung observed 'every single image, every item of my psychic inventory', while striving to 'classify them scientifically' and to 'realize them in actual life' (1962: 218).

In Jung's case, the turbulent and terrifying dialogue between consciousness and the unconscious became a creative process, and eventually led to the emergence of a new psychology. His conclusion was that the aim of the difficult, often dark dialogue between consciousness and the unconscious is to promote self-awareness, and to lead the conscious mind to new realizations about itself, the psyche, and the outside world.

Summary

In Jung's view, the unconscious consists of two layers: the deeper collective level, and the more superficial personal part. The collective unconscious is autonomous and contains universal structures that are the same for all individuals, such as archetypes. Its personal counterpart, which is closer to consciousness and is therefore more accessible, is home to complexes, fantasies, impressions, intuitions and any other hidden material reflecting the life of a particular individual.

Unlike Freud, Jung emphasized the autonomous nature of the unconscious and promoted respect for its contents. For instance, instead of a direct interpretation of symbols as standing for various childhood complexes, he advocated *amplifying* dreams and fantasies. Importantly, they cannot be fully comprehended or controlled, for the conscious mind is only a tip of an iceberg surrounded by the dark waters of the unconscious.

2 Archetypes
Characters

Archetypes and archetypal images

Archetypes are one of several elements of Jungian thought, alongside psychological types that are now firmly embedded in our everyday language and popular culture. Today, we speak of the 'archetypal' politician, villain, survivor or authority figure. The list is endless. But what do we actually mean by 'archetypal' and does Jung's concept of the archetype coincide with today's picture?

When we describe something or someone as 'archetypal', what we actually mean is 'typical' or 'stereotypical', in other words, just like other people or things in a similar group. There may be a pattern, a set of common features. For instance, an archetypal sports car would be a Lamborghini . . . an ostentatious, angular, aggressive-looking sports car, often bright red or yellow, with doors that open upwards. Such a car is made to be noticed, it demands attention. We all recognize these common features when we see the car out in the street, and we all understand that what unites them is this need to attract attention to the owner. We spot cultural patterns: the bleached-blond cinematic villain, the flashy car, the politician who changes his moral values in accordance with the situation, the inflexible bureaucrat who treats people as mere numbers and figures. These are all part of our everyday lives.

The word *archetype* entered English via Latin from Greek *arkhetupon* – 'something moulded first as a model', *arkhe* meaning 'primitive' and *typos* 'a model' (Oxford Dictionary of English, 2006: 81). Now it is probably clear why we keep using this word when we see typical representatives of a group, something that is repeatedly present in our environment.

Jung's definition of the archetype was both different and similar to our popular usage. Clearly, he also liked the idea of a mould, a model, of something that serves as a prototype for all the objects in its class. Unfortunately for us, his definition of the archetype is quite imprecise, and, rather like his amplification method of elucidating dream images, does not presuppose a single encyclopaedic definition, or a clear interpretation, once and for all. Instead, it consists of many complementing definitions, or rather, attempts at describing the phenomenon of archetype. It is very much like building a house by gradually adding layers of bricks.

First of all, Jung assigns the archetypes a dwelling place: they reside in the collective unconscious (CW 9/I: para. 4). In the essay 'Archetypes of the Collective Unconscious', he also launches into a lengthy digression on the history of the archetype, and mentions a diverse range of thinkers who had used the concept before, from the Alexandrian philosopher Philo Judaeus, who lived in the first century AD, to Jung's contemporary, the French anthropologist Lucien Levy-Bruhl (1857–1939), who is responsible for popularizing the term *représentation collectives* (collective representations), or group beliefs shared by all members of a society. Interestingly enough, Jung omits the fact that Levy-Bruhl, in his turn, borrowed the term from the sociologist and philosopher Émile Durkheim (1858–1917).

Later on in his career, Jung decided to distinguish the blobs of psychic matter residing in the darkness of the collective unconscious (archetypes *per se*) from the concrete forms they take when they reach the light of consciousness. Archetypes in their basic state are 'invisible' for consciousness. Yet, they take different guises in particular cultures and in individual minds. The archetype, Jung writes, 'is essentially an unconscious content that is altered by becoming conscious and by being perceived, and it takes its colour from the individual consciousness in which it happens to appear' (CW 9/I: para. 5). In other words, consciousness, or rather, 'conscious elaboration', as Jung calls it, both alter and polish the precious stones they extract from the depths of the unconscious. One needs human consciousness and symbolic imagination to bring them to life.

For instance, the idea of the unachievable psychic unity (the archetype of the self) is so abstract that it is difficult to express in words. However, Jesus Christ as one of the symbolic representations of the self is both relatable and emotionally powerful. The same applies to any other archetypal image of the self, from Dionysos to contemporary cultural images of perfection such as Marvel's superheroes. The archetype is essentially an unconscious content that is altered by becoming conscious and by being recognized, and it takes its colour from the individual consciousness in which it happens to appear' (CW 9/I: 6).

Importantly, the symbolic process 'is an experience *in images and of images*', which is why language may be struggling with describing archetypes and their functions. Thus, archetypal image is born out of the act of perceiving and describing, even though putting archetypal images into words is a strenuous process that somewhat diminishes its numinous power.

Jung discerns a range of archetypes (discussed in more detail later in the chapter): the anima and the animus, the shadow, the hero, the child, the trickster, the old wise woman, the old wise man, and the self. Even from this brief summary, we can see that they cover a whole range of basic yet powerful human experiences: finding a partner (the anima, the animus), dealing with the parents (the old wise figures), being conscious of your negative traits (the shadow), maintaining the balance between being an individual and belonging to society (the trickster), keeping the creativity alive (the child) and, finally, trying to keep together the different parts of the psyche (the self). All archetypes have a positive and negative side to them. For instance, the old wise woman can appear to you in a dream as a witch or as a helpful fairy godmother; and the trickster in fairy tales can be an outlaw or a culture hero. Depending on whether you take the perspective of Zeus or the people who learned to use fire, Prometheus is a criminal who deserves a tortuous punishment for his theft of fire, or a man who led humanity out of darkness and into progress.

Jung goes on to say in 'Archetypes of the Collective Unconscious' that archetypes are nothing less than unconscious contents fleshed out as group beliefs in accordance with a particular culture. These group beliefs take many forms: myth, fairy tale, tribal lore, dreams and fantasies (and even, I dare say, urban mythology expressed in contemporary narratives in film and television). Jung carefully traces this delicate process of 'fleshing out' – the moment when the archetype, a shapeless blob of unconscious material, emerges in the culture or the mind of a dreamer in the shape of a seductive female water spirit, an ugly witch, a helpful elf or an amusing fool.

What do they do and why do we need them?

Why do archetypes exist? Why does the unconscious release these images: all these heroes in fairy tales, the fearsome gods in myths, the figure of the *doppelgänger* (the double) in novels? What do they mean psychologically? Clearly, the unconscious 'thinks' that we need them. This is where the most interesting part starts. 'Archetypally formed ideas' are the symbolic language in which the collective unconscious speaks. They are its 'needful reaction' to the challenges the human psyche faces on 'its' life path (CW 9/I: para. 45). This is because 'the collective unconscious contains . . . an historical mirror-image of the world. It, too, is a world, but a world of images' (CW 7: para. 507).

In her book *The Psychology of C. G. Jung* (1942), Jung's colleague Jolande Jacobi, instead of providing the readers with a straightforward definition of the archetype, focuses more on their function in the life of the individual. Why would the unconscious suddenly show you a nightmare in which you are approached in a dark alley by a gang of street robbers? Or why do you have a recurrent dream of going up in an elevator which does not stop at the floor where you are supposed to get off, and you fear it will eventually crash through the roof? Why do you break down in tears every time you hear a song which leaves other people unaffected? The symbols, images and modes of action with which we deal every day, and which are contained in dreams, visions, songs, contemporary and folk narratives, 'exert a determining influence on psychic life as a whole; they have a dominant functional character and an extremely high energy charge' (1942: 39).

The archetype, according to Jung, has a numinous effect – that is, it is emotionally powerful and overwhelming for the one who is experiencing it. In fact, it is so powerful that it is almost out of human control – 'the subject is gripped by it as though by an instinct'. It is even more potent than an instinct as 'instinct itself can be restrained and even overcome by this power' (CW 5: 225).

Where the conscious mind fails to find a solution to a difficult life situation, the wisdom of the collective psyche, which 'has seen it all before', comes to the rescue. The archetypes are 'reflections of instinctive . . . reactions to certain situations; with their inborn propensities they circumvent consciousness and lead to modes of behaviour which are psychologically necessary though they do not always seem appropriate when considered rationally from without' (1942: 40-1). What Jung and Jacobi actually mean when they describe the role of archetypes in human life and examine the reasons why they appear to us in the form of narratives is that we – and particularly the Western individual, the man of modernity – place so much faith in the ability of our conscious mind to find a solution to complex moral and emotional issues that we forget to listen to our unconscious. Meanwhile, the unconscious does have answers, which it often presents to us as symbols and stories – in a format with which we can relate and identify.

Jacobi also emphasizes that archetypes can take a variety of forms, from static images to actions, processes, reactions and attitudes (1942: 40). In fact, these archetypes designating processes rather than human characters are named by Jung 'the archetypes of transformation'. Their task, he writes, is to represent a transformation on the individuation path: 'Like the personalities, these archetypes are true and genuine symbols that cannot be exhaustively interpreted, either as signs or as allegories' (CW 9/I: para. 80).

For instance, many Russian folk tales start with Ivan the Fool being laughed at by his father, brothers and the entire village in which he lives. He then decides to go and seek his fortune and improve his social prospects, if only to prove to everyone that it is not he who is stupid, it is them because he is the one who gets out there to discover new opportunities while they are stuck at home and are socially conformist. Being 'normal' would not get them anywhere. By the end of the tale, the proactive fool wins a beautiful aristocratic wife and half a kingdom, leaving his cautious neighbours consumed with envy.

In these stories, Ivan the Fool can be seen as either (or both) the hero and the trickster; while his decision to leave his village and seek his fortune in the wider world is an attitude, his journey is a process. Archetypal processes and attitudes drive the story. We recognize these characters and motions as they are present in mythology, folklore and contemporary narratives in very similar ways. The presence of these structures and symbols in narratives is so regular that many people attempted to count the number of all possible typical structures occurring in folk narratives. Among these people were the Russian formalist Vladimir Propp (1895–1970), the American mythologist Joseph Campbell (1904–1987) and the scriptwriting doctor Christopher Vogler (1949–). Vogler's books, in which he uses Jung and Campbell to show the importance of archetypes, both in their character and process forms, in creative writing, are incredibly popular. We will return to them in Chapter 5.

Although Jung and his colleagues paid more attention to archetypal figures than to archetypal processes, it does not mean that processes are less important. For some industries, such as creative writing and screenwriting, the drives and attitudes are as important as 'character' archetypes such as the shadow and the anima.

Their meaning-making properties explain why archetypes are often activated, and become particularly powerful, when the individual cannot see where he or she is going. Suddenly we may start having recurring dreams, or become drawn to certain films or start liking certain kind of books. The goal of this often difficult and overwhelming process is 'illumination of higher consciousness', by means of which the initial situation is 'overcome on a higher level' (CW 9/I: para. 82).

Archetypes and the individuation path: characters and milestones

Archetypes, as Jung envisaged them, are the constituents (as well as stages) in the individuation process. Because they represent different human experiences, they more or less define what it means to be human. Jung singles out a range of archetypes, all corresponding to particular psychological issues in the life of the individual: growing up and leaving the parental home, searching for a relationship and falling in love, dealing with lack of motivation, managing change, etc. There are many others, and indeed it is a point of some debate as to the extent to which the number of archetypes is fixed – certainly, the variation in the images assumed by archetypes seems to be endless and at the same time immediately familiar.

According to the classical Jungian scheme, archetypes are encountered during the individuation process in a particular order. In *The Psychology of C. G. Jung*, Jolande Jacobi outlines the order in which individuals deal with the major archetypes on their individuation path: the shadow, the anima/the animus, the old wise man, the old wise woman, and the self. She does not discuss in detail the trickster or the child. Presumably, this means that we have to deal with them on a regular basis throughout our lives. Contemporary Jungian thinking is more relaxed about the sequence in which archetypes are encountered by the individual, and certainly does not see it as 'fixed'.

The shadow

The shadow archetype is one of the main contributions from Analytical Psychology to popular culture. In fact, Jung and his colleagues often used examples from popular culture and the arts, literature, painting and cinema, to explore the shadow: Caliban from Shakespeare's *The Tempest*, Mr. Hyde from Stevenson's *Strange Case of Dr. Jekyll and Mr. Hyde*, Mary Shelley's Frankenstein monster, and numerous other examples. All these examples are of fiends mistreated and controlled by the people who created them. Or rather, their masters, who treat them with a mixture of fear and disgust, and hide them from the public as something horrible and shameful, are under the false impression of managing their monsters. This deceptive impression cannot be further from the truth. The nameless monster pursues and murders his creator and 'father', Victor Frankenstein; the respectable Victorian gentleman mutates into the perverted Mr. Hyde, who he is no longer able to keep in check; and Caliban, far from being a meek and obedient slave, plots to kill his master Prospero.

In all three stories, the cruelty and moral ugliness of the good citizen and master are transferred onto their counterparts, the treacherous demons. Thus, the master is presented as godlike: courteous, kind, knowledgeable, intelligent and benevolent, while the ogre is brutal, rough and stupid – he is the devil. These examples from literature recreate with great precision the mechanism used by people not willing to acknowledge their negative qualities. They don't want to accept these flaws as part of their personalities. As a result, the rejected character traits, such as jealousy, envy, greed and aggression, become the shadow. The negative qualities are repressed, pushed out of sight, sent back to the unconscious, where they fester and lie in wait for the right moment to jump out and wreak havoc on their unsuspecting carrier. The shadow is the 'dark brother' in whom all the negative aspects of human nature are stored.

The Jungian school saw the encounter with the shadow as the first significant challenge on the way to becoming a self-aware individual.

Bystreetsky: *The shadow*

Jung defines the shadow as primarily 'a moral problem that challenges the whole ego-personality, for no one can become conscious of the shadow without considerable moral effort. To become conscious of it involves recognising the dark aspects of one's personality as present and real' (CW 9/II: para. 14). Echoing the Freudian and post-Freudian description of narcissism as involving looking for a perfect reflection in the mirror, Jung writes about the shadow as a problem of self-image, an issue that inevitably requires confronting the imperfect reflection:

> . . . whoever looks into the mirror of the water will see first of all his own face. Whoever goes to himself risks a confrontation with himself. The mirror does not flatter, it faithfully shows whatever looks into it; namely, the face we never show to the world because we cover it with the *persona*, the mask of the actor. But the mirror lies behind the mask and shows the true face.
>
> (Jung, CW 9/I: 43)

Although the shadow is often depicted in narratives and appears in dreams as a very negative, terrifying figure; as a *doppelgänger* threatening to engulf the individual and take over his or her life, this archetype is extremely important for the individuation process. Like all other archetypes, it has a positive aspect. For instance, it is a source of creativity and the true spirit of life (Jung, 1963: 262). This is a surprising description given the overall negativity surrounding the shadow. It reflects the fact that creativity is raw energy, often born out of conflict and involving strife for perfection. In this sense, the shadow is linked to the figure of the trickster, which also takes part in the generation of creativity (discussed later in the chapter).

A serious problem: the collective shadow

It may sound as if the shadow is exclusively an individual responsibility as it concerns individual character traits such as envy, ambition and competitiveness. But what happens when these traits infect whole nations, or even continents; when wars are started, and ethnic cleansing takes place? Who is to blame: the ideology that issues orders to individual members to send prisoners to a gas chamber, or the individuals themselves who not only fulfil the order but also believe their actions are nothing out of the ordinary, and a morally correct thing to do? In other words, do these terrible actions belong to the personal or the collective shadow?

Jung subdivided the shadow into personal and collective versions in order to describe the mechanism by which people lose themselves in collective thinking and thus lose all individual judgement. The collective version,

Jung emphasizes, is particularly terrifying and incredibly infectious because it emerges when personal negative feelings, propensities and character traits become multiplied and transformed into collective negative behaviour; when hatred, envy and rage are expressed on a mass scale. This is why it is important to recognize and deal with one's own small shadow lest it become seduced by the power of the mass:

> It is a frightening thought that man also has a shadow side to him, consisting not just of little weaknesses and foibles, but of a positively demonic dynamism. The individual seldom knows anything of this; to him, as an individual, it is incredible that he should ever in any circumstances go beyond himself. But let these harmless creatures form a mass, and there emerges a raging monster; and each individual is only one tiny cell in the monster's body, so that for better or worse he must accompany it on its bloody rampages and even assist it to the utmost. Having a dark suspicion of these grim possibilities, man turns a blind eye to the shadow-side of human nature. Blindly he strives against the salutary dogma of original sin, which is yet so prodigiously true. Yes, he even hesitates to admit the conflict of which he is so painfully aware.
>
> (CW 7: 35)

The shadow, Marie-Louise von Franz writes, is:

> exposed to collective inflections to a much greater extent that is the conscious personality. When a man is alone . . . he feels relatively all right; but as soon as "the others" do dark, primitive things, he begins to fear that if he does not join in, he will be considered a fool. Thus he gives way to the impulses that do not really belong to him at all.
>
> (Jung & von Franz, 1964: 175)

One cannot get rid of the shadow entirely, but one can learn to manage it. As such, it is an important part of the individuation process. As Christopher Hauke notes in *Jung and the Postmodern*, for Jung, individuation means integrating neglected parts of the psyche:

> including parts of oneself that have been lost or neglected not only due to circumstances or personal history – parents, upbringing and so on – but have also been lost or neglected due to the collective conditions of the era and culture [. . .] However, the personal and the collective, as well as the past and the present, are difficult to differentiate and separate in any final way.
>
> (Hauke, 2000: 109)

The shadow is frequently present in both cinematic and television narratives, which often employ this archetype to show the split personality of a contemporary individual. For instance, Tyler Durden (Brad Pitt) in *Fight Club* (1999, directed by David Fincher) is the nameless protagonist's *doppelgänger* who represents his repressed, split-off personality traits. Tyler is a social terrorist who professes his disdain towards society, and who does everything the narrator does not dare to do: urinates in the food at restaurants where he works as a waiter; makes soap out of liposuction fat and sells it to posh perfumeries; destroys an Apple store; and has outrageous sex with the protagonist's girlfriend Marla (Helena Bonham Carter). As the film progresses, the double gets madder and more dangerous in his plans to destroy the global financial system while the spineless protagonist makes half-hearted attempts to control his runaway 'second nature'. Like many *doppelgänger* narratives, the film ends with the protagonist killing his double, nearly dying himself as a result (because the shadow is an inseparable part of human nature; one cannot just 'kill it off'), and redeeming the world by releasing it from the grip of capitalist greed and globalization.

The anima and the animus

In the classical model of the individuation process, after the encounter with the shadow, the questor has to deal with the anima or the animus – the 'soul image' of the opposite sex defining our romantic relationships. Jung called these soul-image figures 'the anima' (in men) and 'the animus' (in women). These figures remain with us throughout our lives and more or less determine our romantic involvements and choice of partners (CW 7: para. 296). We fall in love with people who resemble our 'soul image'. We also mistake real people for our anima/animus, having projected familiar characteristics onto them. The animus and anima play tricks on us. For instance, we may keep falling for the same type of person over and over again, regardless of the fact that our relationship with this type never works out.

In myths and fairy tales, these archetypal images can be presented in both their positive (helping, kindly, useful) and negative (demonic) incarnations. As a rule, men have to deal with two types of anima: domestic and passive ('the angel') and proactive and intellectual ('the whore'). Men possessed by their anima become 'moody' and 'dominated by feminine drives' (Jacobi, 1942: 115). Meanwhile, women are endowed with more than one animus, and they form a sort of chorus of internal voices. These 'animuses' may make the woman 'argumentative', 'opinionated', and prone to 'masculine' reactions (1942: 115).

Jung was particularly interested in the anima's ability to inspire the man, and often conflated the anima with the real woman onto whom the anima is

Bystreetsky: *The anima*

projected. In his view, women should serve as inspiration for men because 'woman, with her dissimilar psychology, has been a source of information about things for which a man has no eyes' (CW 7: para. 296). By this, Jung means that a female, being by nature more emotional and sensual, has a better relationship with the unconscious, and often pays for this special connection by being 'less rational' than a male.

Unfortunately, this extremely conservative view, which does not take into consideration different kinds of gender identities, is echoed by other Jungian writers, even the female ones, including Jolande Jacobi and Marie-Louise von Franz. Both have written about 'opinionated', animus-possessed women who dare to express their views, and about men influenced by their anima to the extent of becoming 'moody' and 'receptive to the irrational' (Jung, 1964: 186). This view has since been challenged by many post-Jungians, including Andrew Samuels and Susan Rowland (see the Bibliography).

The old wise man and the old wise woman

Parents form our vision of the world. They are the most influential figures in a child's life. Even as we grow up, Jung writes, they remain imprinted upon our minds, eventually turning into 'spirits', or 'alien elements'; into kinds of internalized voices (CW 7: para. 296). We do not necessarily see these voices as part of us or even as belonging to our parents. These ghost-like figures become 'increasingly shut away from consciousness, and on account of the restrictive influence they sometimes continue to exert, they easily acquire a negative aspect' (CW 7: para. 296).

When we call ourselves stupid for making a mistake, or, on the contrary, praise ourselves for a small achievement, we often speak about our actions in our parents' words. Sometimes they appear to us as anthropomorphic figures: the old wise man and the old wise woman. Jung also used the Polynesian word *mana* (authority, prestige) to describe their powerful influence on us. The mana-personalities become prominent, Jacobi writes, after we have dealt with the major issues associated with the animus and the anima (Jacobi, 1942: 124). Again, this is a very linear and restrictive view of the individuation process, as it prescribes the individual to deal with his or her issues in a certain order. In reality, the individuation process does not necessarily have to have a certain sequence in which self-discoveries happen.

Like any archetypes, these figures have positive and negative guises. The old wise man, who often materializes in fairy tales in the form of a magician, father figure or helpful (or evil) elf, stands for spiritual meaning, and often brings to the ailing or confused hero some clarification of his or her desperate situation. This archetype, Jung writes, represents 'knowledge, reflection, insight, wisdom, cleverness, and intuition on the one hand, and on the other, moral qualities such as goodwill and readiness to help, which make his "spiritual" character sufficiently plain' (Jung, CW 9/I: 406). Yet, in its negative incarnation, it may appear as a wicked villain who 'does evil for evil's sake': a ruthless king, a concocter of poisons or a horrid water spirit. This ambivalence reflects the dynamic character of the psyche in which nothing is ever set in stone, all views are relative and should be balanced out by the opposite. 'Too much of a good thing' can also be bad.

Similarly, the wise old woman can appear to the protagonist as a helpful motherly figure or a wicked witch, and can symbolize now 'wisdom and spiritual exaltation' and 'helpful instinct and impulse that . . . cherishes and sustains', and now 'anything secret, hidden, dark; the abyss, the world of the dead, anything that devours, seduces and poisons' (CW 9/I: para. 158). The mother is ambivalent as she is both 'the loving and the terrible mother' (CW 9/I: para. 158). Continuing Jung's conservative (or even sexist) tradition of endowing anthropomorphic female archetypes with 'earthly' and 'feminine' qualities, Jacobi argues that the old wise woman, or the great mother, is linked to the earthly qualities such as 'the material principle' and 'the cold, impersonal truth of nature' (1942: 125), while the old wise man symbolizes the high, celestial phenomena such as spiritual development and searching for a meaning in life.

As symbols, the old wise man and the old wise woman go way beyond the literal meaning (our actual parents), and help us express and process maturation issues: growing up, finding our identity, choosing our path, as well as getting in trouble and looking for help during the individuation process. These 'wise' archetypes, despite the possibility of them turning into evil figures, represent the ability of the psyche to self-direct, self-train and self-heal. For instance, Luke Skywalker in *Star Wars* (1977, directed by George Lucas) is advised by Obi-Wan Kenobi, but also externally motivated by Darth Vader, the two father figures illuminating the two sides of the protagonist's own nature and guiding him towards better self-understanding and self-reflection.

The child

The child is the staple archetype in mythological and religious narratives in which it is usually presented as having superhuman abilities, being chased by evil people, and miraculously surviving numerous accidents to become a superstar. Dionysos, Heracles, Jesus, Osiris and Horus (the son of Isis and Osiris who went on to avenge his father's death at the hands of Osiris' brother Seth) all loosely fit into this pattern. The archetype is also popular

Bystreetsky: *The old wise man*

Bystreetsky: *The old wise woman*

among contemporary novelists and screenwriters who gave us Peter Pan, Harry Potter and Edward Scissorhands, to name but a few.

Unlike the shadow and the anima/animus duo, the archetype of the child is tricky to define. In fact, in the essay 'The Psychology of the Child Archetype', Jung 'amplified' it instead of giving it a clear definition. First of all, the archetype provides a link between our past and our future. On the one hand, it symbolizes a picture of 'certain *forgotten* things in our childhood', and represents the preconscious aspect of the collective psyche (CW 9/I: para. 273). As a rule, his birth (for this is usually a male child which reflects the patriarchal nature of many cultures) is unusual. He is a child of a god or a goddess, and in many cases his high-status parents prefer to remain anonymous. This element of the motif implies that a godlike infant cannot be produced by ordinary parents; surely his unusual abilities are inherited from very special people. Yet, despite his special abilities and influential parents, the child's life is fraught with danger. He has merciless and ruthless enemies: for instance, the goddess Hera who tried to destroy the unborn Dionysos out of jealousy because he was the child of Zeus and a mortal woman, Semele; or King Herod, who according to the Gospel of Matthew, ordered the murder of all the infants in Bethlehem hoping that the baby Jesus would be among them.

The child is our connection with the past, with the forgotten world of innocence in which our creativity was unfettered and we felt boundlessly powerful. That is, before the world of adult responsibility fully descended upon us. Reality does limit creative impulses and restrains the flight of the imagination. Sometimes we dream of being children again, or going back to our childhood home, nursery, or school. The archetype of the child keeps alive the creative impulse in us while also nurturing the inner purity and fragility that makes us believe in magic, in the impossible: 'In every adult there lurks a child – an eternal child, something that is always becoming, is never completed, and calls for unceasing care, attention and education. That is the part of the human personality which wants to develop and become whole' (CW 17: para. 286).

The link with this innocent past before the full arrival of reality is vitally important for the feeling of being alive, of being able to accomplish things; for the background feeling of having these residual, hidden superpowers. This is, on the other hand, how the archetype also points to the future, to all the possible accomplishments and achievements of which we are capable if we keep the child inside alive. In mythology, the child is a future hero, and many mythological saviours are child gods. In the individuation process, the wonder-child 'paves the way for a future change of personality' and 'anticipates the figure that comes from the synthesis of conscious and unconscious elements in the personality. It is therefore a symbol which unites the opposites; a mediator, bringer of healing, that is, one who makes whole' (Jung, 1951, CW 9/I: 278). In myths, the (usually male) child prodigy possesses miraculous abilities: he can casually kill dangerous snakes as he lays in his cot (Heracles), survive numerous assassination attempts like Dionysus, or, like Harry Potter, play a trick or two on the evil members of his adopted family.

Jung theorizes that the child motif corresponded to the birth of the personality and its development and eventual survival in the world. It represents the 'infancy' of the individuation process, its fragile, humble beginnings. Growing out of the unconscious, and into an unsafe world, is a heroic process. The hero-ego, the conscious psyche, 'emerges' from the primeval darkness, and tries to establish itself in its surroundings and to gain a unique identity. Attainment of a recognizable personality marks the birth of the individual as someone separate from the crowd, as well as someone relatively independent from the collective unconscious, from 'mother nature':

> The Hero's main feat is to overcome the monster of darkness: it is the long-hoped-for and expected triumph of consciousness over the unconscious. [. . .] The coming of consciousness was probably the most tremendous experience of primeval times, for with it a world came into being whose existence no one had suspected before. 'And God said: "Let there be light!"' is the projection of that immemorial separation of the conscious from the unconscious. [. . .] Hence the 'child' distinguishes itself by deeds which point to the conquest of the dark.
>
> (CW 9/I: 284)

Another interesting aspect of the archetype firmly present in both ancient and contemporary narratives is that the child is often abandoned, neglected, lost, exposed to all kinds of dangers, or his parents simply die, and he has to use his miraculous survival skills (or develop them) in order to overcome difficulties and to triumph over his enemies (most of whom want him dead). Contemporary authors and filmmakers are particularly fascinated with this aspect of the archetype. For instance, Harry Potter's real parents are murdered by Lord Voldemort, and his step-parents keep him in the cupboard under the stairs. Similarly, Tim Burton's characters have a whole range of dysfunctional childhoods, usually parentless, or parentless in the metaphorical sense. This includes Edward Scissorhands, whose father collapses and dies before completing his son's hands (*Edward Scissorhands*, 1993); Willy Wonka, whose weird behaviour and reclusiveness reflect his tortured upbringing in the hands of a sadistic dentist father (*Charlie and the Chocolate Factory*, 2005); and Alice from *Alice in Wonderland* (2010),

Bystreetsky: *The child*

who has only distant (and fond) memories of her father while her mother treats her as an object that has to achieve a certain social status for the family. His two most recent films also concern orphans or children who look like orphans: *Big Eyes* (2014) and *Miss Peregrine's Home for Peculiar Children* (2016).

The child's specialness is twinned with the abandonment motif which is an integral aspect of the child myth because, translated back into the language of individual development, it symbolizes personal independence, even when it has been achieved through isolation and hardship. Abandonment, Jung writes, is necessary because it triggers the birth of the individual as a separate entity (CW 9/I: 285). Moreover, the child

> is all that is abandoned and exposed and at the same time divinely powerful; the insignificant, dubious beginning, and the triumphant end. The 'eternal child' in man is an indescribable experience, an incongruity, a handicap, and a divine prerogative; an imponderable that determines the ultimate worth or worthlessness of a personality.
>
> (CW 9/I: 300)

The child is a future hero, a future individual, and becoming an individual is a difficult task.

The hero

The hero is one of the most relatable archetypes, and one of the easiest to define. Basically, it symbolizes the individuating, progressing human being whose everyday struggle with life and reality is metaphorically presented in the form of superhuman tasks such as dragon-slaying, maiden-saving and magical transformations. The myth of the hero, Jung writes, 'is first and foremost a self-representation of the longing of the unconscious, of its quenched and unquenchable desire for the light of consciousness' (CW 5: para. 299). Throughout his texts, Jung examines various hero figures, from the predictable characters from the Bible (Noah, Jesus) and world mythology (Rama from the Sanskrit epic *The Ramayana*, the Egyptian Osiris) to his favourite characters from classical and contemporary literature such as Goethe's Faust or James Joyce's Ulysses.

Human decisions, events and milestones are encased into metaphors and symbols – archetypal images, the language of the unconscious, which may know a little more than you do when it comes to finding a solution to a difficult situation. It presents it to you in the form of an archetypal narrative, constructing a detailed visual-narrative canvas out of the range of universal details – archetypal images, situations, attitudes and actions. Everyday life can be a struggle, and it helps to see it as an externalized 'heroic' narrative, as a symbolic story in which making up with an oppressive parent is presented as slaying a dragon, and spring-cleaning the house as cleaning the Augean stables. Everyone is a hero with a reserve of superhuman power, fighting through life's ups and downs.

Jung calls the hero 'the finest of all symbols of the libido' because of its exceptional clarity and transparency, with which it transforms from the blob of psychic energy that is the pure archetype into an archetypal image:

> Here the symbolism leaves the objective, material realm of astral and meteorological images and takes on human form, changing into a figure who passes from joy to sorrow, from sorrow to joy, like the sun, now stands high at the zenith and now is plunged into darkest night, only to rise again in new splendor.
>
> (CW 5: para. 251)

Not surprisingly, there is an abundance of superheroes and heroines in contemporary mythology – comic books, television and Hollywood cinema. Men and women with superpowers – Batman, Superman, Spider Man, Wonder Woman and Catwoman – battle with the personal and social issues plaguing the individual today, from urban crime and pollution to loneliness and loss of community. These contemporary manifestations of the hero archetype will be discussed in more detail in Chapter 3.

The trickster

The trickster is probably the most intriguing archetype. It has attracted serious attention from specialists outside the field of Analytical Psychology: sociologists, anthropologists and folklorists. Most mythological canons have a trickster character: a fool, a clown, a rebel, a prankster, or a village idiot who does the opposite of what the other residents of the village consider normal, and is therefore everyone's laughing stock.

The trickster's dislike for what we humans call 'the norm' is ingrained in the guises he takes (for it is often a male, and only occasionally a female): animals, birds, creatures that lack a stable human form. Many mythological and folkloric tricksters are animals, and even when they are not, some association with the animal kingdom is often present. The African trickster club boasts a spider (Kwaku Anansi), a hare, and a tortoise; the Northern American group includes a raven, a coyote, a rabbit and Wakdjunkaga's numerous animal transformations. The fox is the principal trickster of Russian fairy tales; India has the monkey called Hanuman (one of the heroes of Ramayana); the best-known Chinese trickster is also a monkey – the hero of the novel *The Journey To the West* (1590); in Peruvian fairy tales, the trickster's role is played by a guinea pig; Argentinean folklore has Tokwah, who is neither human nor animal; Japanese folktales mention Hare and Badger as cunning transformers.

There are other ways of challenging the *status quo* than being an animal or a half-animal. Many trickster figures are thieves (Hermes), dangerous revolutionaries (Prometheus) or evil pranksters (Wakdjunkaga from the Winnebago folklore). There are a number of features which unite all these diverse characters: they love breaking boundaries, shapeshifting and gender-bending, challenging the existing order of things, showing off their total disregard for authority, making silly and lewd jokes, and engaging in all kinds of shameless and antisocial behaviours. It is not unusual for a trickster to have sex in public, steal treasure from a god or use a king's private chapel as a toilet (and then convince the king that it's a gift from god).

The trickster, Jung writes in his essay 'On the Psychology of the Trickster Figure' is both 'subhuman and superhuman, a bestial and divine being, whose chief and most alarming characteristic is his unconsciousness' (CW 9/I: 472). It is a creature of the unconscious, the wise fool, the clown and the delight-maker. He has a dual nature: half-animal, half divine. Tricksters reverse the hierarchic order, are shapeshifters, and are famous for their malicious tricks and pranks. Jung also mentions the strong link between the trickster figure and the tradition of carnival, where the Devil appeared as *simia dei* – the ape of God (CW 9/I: 465–472). It also 'is a faithful reflection of an absolutely undifferentiated human consciousness, corresponding to a psyche that has hardly left the animal level' (CW 9/I: 471).

The highest meaning of this archetype is in the management of the relationship between personal and social elements in the life of the individual. Essentially, the trickster symbolizes human ability to manage and process change as well as to adapt to the environment. By showing the middle finger to the gods and kings, the trickster insists on the right of the individual to make decisions instead of being dependent on the system for guidance. All people are unique individualities and yet they are also part of a whole hierarchy of communities, from basic (family, school, urban area) to the highest level involving culture and nation. The trickster is responsible for maintaining the balance between these two spheres of the individual's life. Because the individuation process also involves maintaining the balance between these two spheres, the trickster is one of the key elements of the individuation process. It is also one of the driving forces of this process, pushing the individual towards a better understanding of his or her place in society.

Bystreetsky: *The trickster*

The self

The self (also discussed in Chapter 4) is not just a personality component – it is also an archetype. It stands for never-achievable psychological wholeness. People need the concept of the self, Marie-Louise von Franz explains, because they can never be satisfied with mere existing and surviving; they need to know that there is a higher purpose to being human. The self provides this purpose 'above and beyond' the basic drives (Jung, 1964: 215). This archetype is 'a living mystery that can be expressed only as a symbol, and for its expression the unconscious often chooses the powerful image of the Cosmic Man', that is, a god-like, omnipresent, gigantic being 'who embraces and contains the whole cosmos' (1964: 211–15).

Humankind traditionally expressed the idea of perfection in the figures of gods and heroes – creatures with superhuman abilities and magical skills. Externalized as a perfect god or goddess (for instance, Buddha, Christ or Gaia), the self becomes a site onto which we place our hopes and fears, or, to use a proper psychotherapeutic term, onto which we *project* thoughts and emotions. The archetype, however, does not necessarily have to take human-like (anthropomorphic) guises: that is, wise men or women. It may appear to us as a stone or a helpful animal (a monkey, a wolf or a she-bear) guiding the dreamer or the protagonist of a narrative towards a greater self-understanding (1964: 221). The alchemical philosopher's stone, which (it was thought) could turn simple substances into gold, is probably one of its most popular manifestations. It is still present today in popular literature and film.

In narratives, the self is the driving force of the story, and the protagonist's main motivation vehicle. The idea of a hero's journey is to bring the quester nearer to this unity, the psychic perfection that eliminates all conflicts and problems. Although the achievement of this inner peace and absolute perfection is impossible, during the journey the hero attempts to solve at least some of the problems, such as dealing with the shadow, or coming to terms with the animus.

The archetype of the alien

Archetypal images are culture-specific, that is, archetypes are sufficiently flexible to take the shapes specific to a particular society in a particular era. For instance, in our technogenic civilization, one of the most popular archetypal manifestations is the alien. It is everywhere, from films and television to conspiracy theories, children's toys and fancy-dress parties. Extra-terrestrial invaders have dominated science fiction and horror genres even since Georges Méliès *Trip to the Moon* (1902), and their firm presence

Bystreetsky: *The self*

in moving-image narratives was mirrored in the UFO obsession and invasion fantasies that proved enduring in popular imagination throughout the twentieth century. So why is it here? What does it mean to us?

The alien is not, of course, a 'traditional' archetype, and Jung did not include it into his roster of principal symbolic figures that individuals encounter on their way towards self-enlightenment. He did, however, devote a separate essay to it which he called 'Flying Saucers: A Modern Myth of Things Seen in the Sky' (1958), particularly because, in the middle of the twentieth century, sightings of flying saucers and extra-terrestrial creatures became sufficiently widespread to be considered a mass phenomenon. When something so inexplicable and unverifiable happens on such a grand scale, it is bound to attract the interest of psychologists.

Jung was very attuned to the symbols coming from the collective unconscious, to its mass manifestations. The alien was one of these psychic products. After World War II, Jung noticed the growing number of what he called 'visionary rumours' of UFO sightings. Moreover, the press was also full of them, and some of his patients saw flying saucers in dreams. Jung summarizes the incidents in 'Flying Saucers: A Modern Myth of Things Seen in the Sky':

> Nobody knows what they are looking for, or what they want to observe. [. . .] Sometimes they appear to be up to 500 yards in diameter, sometimes small as electric lamps. There are large motherships from which little UFOs slip out or in which they take shelter. They are said to be both manned and unmanned, and in the latter case are remote-controlled. According to the rumour, the occupants are about three feet high and look like human beings, or, conversely, are utterly unlike us. Other reports speak of giants fifteen feet high. They are beings who are carrying out a cautious survey of the earth and considerably avoid all encounters with men, or, more menacingly, are spying out landing places with a view to settling the population of a planet that has got into difficulties and colonizing the earth by force.
>
> (Jung, 2002: 4–5)

By the 1950s, alien invasion had already become a collective dream theme, with people reporting cases of spotting shiny globes in the sky, being abducted by aliens; of extra-terrestrials carving out patterns on crops, or aliens sharing wisdom with their 'less intelligent brothers'. In fact, the figure's ambiguity – its unpredictability and aggression offset by advanced intellect and superhuman abilities – make it an ambivalent projection of humanity's battle with its own shadow.

Jung wrote his essay on this in the 1950s, but the stories of alien invasion have not really changed much since; they have become only more firmly rooted in popular imagination. Alien invasion is a good umbrella metaphor that covers a whole set of contemporary anxieties. The alien figure possesses distinct characteristics: it is highly intelligent, mysterious, omniscient, confident and can read minds. These features render themselves particularly well to the stock sci-fi themes of mind control, conspiracy and paranoia – the traditional sublimation of political fears of such a diverse scope as totalitarian communist governments, capitalist mind-manipulation, colonialist occupation, the hidden power of the media, secret service conspiracies, and other forms of 'big brother' control and surveillance. Not surprisingly, the theme of alien invasion is closely linked to conspiracy theories and to rumours that governments are hiding information about extra-terrestrial visitors. Such conspiracy theories and their accompanying paranoid and persecutory effects are also commonplace fantasies for people with borderline personalities. In turn, this suggests the proximity of these fantasies to the collective unconscious.

Jung had his own explanation of the alien obsession phenomenon. In his essay, he explores a number of UFO sightings, and compares them to similar psycho-spiritual experiences that took place in the Middle Ages. The collective unconscious, as we remember, looks for suitable symbols to express itself. These symbols (archetypal images) are culturally determined, unlike their core contents (archetypes). Jung suggests that the image of the spaceship is the contemporary version of the archetype of the self – the psychological unity, the image of god-like perfection that we aim to become but will never achieve. The UFOs became a powerful mass dream image partly because, in Jung's words, 'anything that looks technological goes down without difficulty with modern man' (CW 10: para. 624).

Jung explains the round shape of flying saucers in terms of universal religious symbolism; in his view, 'the circular symbols have played an important role in every age [. . .] There is an old saying that "God is a circle whose centre is everywhere and circumference nowhere". God in his omniscience, omnipotence, and omnipresence is a totality symbol *par excellence*, something round, complete, and perfect. [. . .] On the antique level, therefore, the UFOs could easily be conceived as "gods"' (CW 10: para. 622).

Even after the two World Wars, Jung argues, there was still a belief in people's intrinsic goodness and the power of human consciousness to control its animal impulses. This belief 'thrust itself to the forefront in the form of a symbolic rumour, accompanied and reinforced by the appropriate visions', and therefore activated an archetype 'that has always expressed order, deliverance, salvation and wholeness' (CW 10: para. 624). In contemporary

Bystreetsky: *The alien – a contemporary version of the self*

Western society, Jung writes somewhat optimistically, 'consciously rationalistic enlightenment predominates' and that 'belief in this world and in the power of man has, despite assurances to the contrary, become an . . . irrefragable truth' (CW 10: para. 623). Every age has its symbols reflecting the same eternal conflicts and universal problems. The UFO thus becomes a saviour, a Christ-like visitor coming to planet Earth to redeem its inhabitants from themselves; or, alternatively, in the form of the angry God from the Old Testament, punishing human beings for their sins and wrongdoings.

In the past fifty years, the alien has become such a stock feature in television and cinema that it has transcended its 'alienness'. Comedies about visitors from outer space, such as *Mars Attacks!* (2000), the *Men in Black* (1997–2012) franchise, *My Stepmother is an Alien* (1988; Richard Benjamin), *Spaceballs* (1987; Mel Brooks) and *Paul* (2011; Greg Mottola), prove that we are prepared to laugh at ourselves, our incompleteness and our dreams of god-like 'perfection'.

Some cinematic aliens invade from the inside by stealing human minds and invading their bodies; others arrive on Earth openly and destroy its cities by fire. Monsters from the *Alien* franchise (1979–1997, directed by Ridley Scott, James Cameron, David Fincher and Jean-Pierre Jeunet) would belong to the first group; and mass invaders from *Independence Day* (1996), directed by Roland Emmerich, Tim Burton's *Mars Attacks!* (1996), Steven Spielberg's *The War of the Worlds* (2005) or *Edge of Tomorrow* (2014, Doug Liman). In both the narrative types, human beings lose control over themselves and their habitat while a more powerful force takes over. The alien has almost been recognized as a projection, as a vessel onto which humans project their fears of themselves, and their hope that the higher nature in them may prevail over the dark impulses and traits.

Summary

Archetypes are the language in which the unconscious speaks to us. When they reach consciousness, archetypes transform from blobs of psychic content into figures, attitudes and processes to help us understand ourselves and the world around us. This is how the unconscious makes itself known to us, and helps us make meaning of the world. As part of the individuation process, archetypal characters and processes cover a comprehensive range of human experiences, from falling in love to keeping alive the creative impulse. Being regular and universal, being shared by all in equal measure on the level of the collective unconscious, archetypes play an important role in the processes that help people explain and organize their existence.

3 The individuation process
The story

Individuation: an overview

We all want to make sense of our world, our emotions and experiences, and our communication with other human beings. Perhaps the easiest way to do this is through stories: fairy tales, myths, novels, TV shows and films. In narratives, we can see our lives – events, circumstances, relationships – as if projected onto the screen, as if reflected in a mirror. Feelings, emotions, fears and anxieties we cannot recognize in ourselves are much easier to see in other people – or better even, in fictional characters. We can see our path clearer when its elements are shown to us from a distance, played out by someone else.

Jung had a special term for the path: the individuation process, or the process of becoming oneself. To individuate means to become an individual – someone undivided, at peace with themselves, aware of their feelings, emotions and character traits, and knowing what they want from life. On the other hand, it also means being aware of your environment – being part of society, of social structures; getting on with other people, if necessary at the detriment of your own interests.

In this sense, the individuation process does not imply being self-centred – rather, it translates into a balance between the personal and the social. Its idea is that the individual learns to make personal choices while also taking others into consideration. In other words, one cannot be an independent person at the expense of society – one can only become an individual *within* society, with its rules and regulations. Individuation, Jung explains, 'does not shut one out from the world, but gathers the world to oneself' (CW 8: para. 432).

Individuation is a living narrative with the sole protagonist as its centre; a plot skeleton of events guided by the protagonist's motivations and goals. Narratives are pre-genre, Swales argues, and 'operate through a framework of temporal succession in which at least some of the events are reactions to previous events' (Swales, 1993: 61). Moreover, they are 'strongly orientated towards the agents of the events being described, rather than to the events themselves' (1993: 61). Bordwell (2007) also defines narrative as a 'contingent universal of human experience. It cuts across distinctions of art and science, fiction and nonfiction, literature and the other arts.' In other words, the central character gives a narrative its internal (meaning) and external (sequential) cohesion, and links the events via determination and purpose. As a narrative, individuation is a structure that can form the base of any genre, and may be elaborated according to the author's needs and aims.

In life and therapy, individuation is also mostly a creative, spontaneous process, a 'natural process within the psyche' that is 'potentially present in every man, although most men are unaware of it' (Jacobi, 1942: 107). We are all protagonists in our own individuation narrative, and the fact that our paths are unique makes our existence meaningful and worth exploring: all life, Jung writes, 'is bound to individual carriers who realize it, and it is simply inconceivable without them. But every carrier is charged with an individual destiny and destination, and the realization of these alone makes sense of life' (CW 15: para. 330). By contrast, in writing, one has to freeze this process in a definitive timeline (although, by way of rebelling against these constraints, some authors offer multiple plot options and several conclusions).

But what is the force that pushes the protagonist to go on a journey and drives her or him towards the goal? The individuation process is driven by what Jung called the centre of personality – the self – which stands for psychological wholeness and a freedom from all worldly conflicts and peace with oneself. This centre is more of a guideline and a phantom rather than something that can be really achieved. The reason why we are capable of multiple journeys which link together into one long 'life journey' is this unattainability of perfection. One can dream of achieving wholeness, but it might never happen. There is nothing tragic in this state of things, however. Having inner conflicts is only human, and while it is possible to integrate some of the issues, it is not possible to get rid of them completely. Arguably, nor is it entirely desirable as the resolution of psychological conflict is one of the spurs to creativity. Meanwhile, narratives show us our unique problems while, at the same time, making us realize that we do not suffer alone, and that our problems are as personal as they are universal.

Unlike Freudian psychology, which is backward-looking and searches for answers to present problems in the individual's past, Jungian theory is more about the future: it is about evaluating one's present position in life and trying to plan the future with this knowledge. The past is important, but not decisive. One learns about oneself as one goes along the path of life, and this process is progressive and aimed at the attainment of psychological wholeness. Although this wholeness can never be fully achieved, one could – in theory – approach some kind of peace with oneself; a pact with one's psyche by appeasing the inner demons. If not peace, individuation offers the potential for a state of equanimity with ourselves, how we are in the world and the ability to cope with the challenges and difficulties of everyday life.

There is nothing wrong with having inner demons, though – indeed, they are unavoidable. Everyone individuates, and, since human beings share the collective unconscious, we all have similar individuation milestones. These milestones are expressed in metaphors and metaphorical situations – or archetypes and archetypal situations, as Jung preferred to call them. All human beings have issues with parents or parental figures; they grow up, struggle with undesirable character traits such as envy, greed and aggression, deal with instincts and sexuality, try to find path and place in life, look for love and acceptance, and try to achieve something significant before death. In other words, individuation is the basic skeleton which is then filled out with personal details: all parents (and the issues associated with them) are different; and the ways in which human beings experience sexual feelings are also very individual. Cinematic narratives provide frameworks for reflecting on a variety of individuation moments, and, as the interaction with the screen is one-way, they are also pliable canvasses for one's fantasies and projections. They are ideal providers of objects for one's individuation narrative.

Individuation in narratives: structure and content

How does individuation translate into creative writing? Well, the narrative is a sort of mediated individuation process – a story (visual or non-visual) outlining the progress of the individual. The type of the progress depends on the genre and plot details. In moving image narratives, this is further complicated by choices presented by creative choices made by various directors and producers, including choice of actors, *mis-en-scène*, camera movement, lighting, framing, editing, etc.

In a story, the individuation becomes the protagonist's path. Individuation of a human being is all about becoming oneself in a given environment. Screenplays and stories are about the protagonist's struggle to find themselves and to find meaning in existence. We watch films and read books precisely because narratives serve as mirrors for our own individuation journey. They show us the possible ways of dealing with things, the alternative turns that can be taken on our path, the various results from decisions that can be made. When we are watching a screen narrative, it is as if we are living our lives through someone else's failures and successes. It helps us understand ourselves, our past, present and future.

Film critics traditionally see Jungian psychology as a source of structural devices such as the individuation/hero myth and the archetypes that are its contents. Imperfect as it is, Christopher Vogler's book *The Writer's Journey* clearly showed the applicability of Jungian Theory for both screenwriting and film criticism. The individuation process is essentially an optimistic concept that presupposes a certain degree of balance, progressivity, maturation and hope in an individual's life. We have this for ourselves, and we also find it appealing when it is reflected in cinematic narratives. This too is what we want to see in films – a story, a development, a progression, a tale of transformation. Individuation – the hero myth – is an ideal metaphor for the description of psychological transformation in a person's life.

Educational goals

The individuation process is, essentially, educational. Human beings have the capacity to learn from narratives; all kinds of narratives: novels, TV series, films, video games, plays, myths, fairy tales. We learn both by reading and watching the stories, and by participating in them: when playing a video game, for instance, or by taking part in an amateur play. We can learn as much from Sid Meier's *Civilization* or the BBC's *Blue Planet* or *Planet Earth* documentary series as we do from an original drama series or something like the *Star Wars* franchise. By storytelling, other people share with us insights into human behaviour and psychology. For instance, the listeners of the Winnebago trickster cycle and other Native American trickster stories were learning about the very foundations of civilized existence, but this learning process was accompanied by humour and laughter. Our task is not just to be entertained, but also to imbibe the wisdom contained in the stories created for us by others.

We merge with the narratives and go through sequences which we may encounter later on in life. We project our own issues onto the stories, and equally introject the material contained in them to form our own experiential wisdom. In other words, we learn from someone struggling, making mistakes, going through difficulties, working out successful strategies, and solving issues. We learn from seeing others try and lose; or try and win. And narratives allows us to do this safely, engaging us while at the same time emphasizing the distance between fantasy and reality. We know that a film does not represent reality; that even a virtual-reality game does not represent reality – it is an enhanced copy of it, but it is still a game. You can get out of a game, but you cannot get out of reality. Narratives are a safe way of exploring the world and its dangers, and they teach by entertaining. We learn from them incessantly, unstoppably, for we are programmed to improve our knowledge of the world by carefully observing it and optimizing our chances of surviving and succeeding.

Every encounter that happens within a narrative is also educational in two ways:

- It makes one learn about oneself (by empathizing with the protagonist, by using the story as a mirror, by examining one's reactions to the story).
- It allows one to learn more about one's environment and community (by testing out various solutions to problems; by testing the boundary between the personal and the social, or between one's own interests and intentions, and the intentions of others).

These two educational functions merge into one: by immersing ourselves into narratives, we develop as a personalities while being aware of our environment and taking it into consideration when making individual decisions. Combined, they constitute the two aspects of the individuation process: balancing individual interests with social rules and requirements.

The three central issues posed in narratives

Traditionally, Analytical Psychology has been discussing nine archetypes: the shadow, the anima, the animus, the child, the trickster, the old wise man (father), the old wise woman (mother), the hero and the self. This book is discussing the same nine archetypes, but does not arrange them in any order the way, for instance, Jolande Jacobi did: the shadow is the first archetype to be encountered by the protagonist, followed by the anima, then the parental figures, and so on, while the final goal of the individuation process is the self.

Moreover, it will be argued that the widely accepted idea of the 'hero's journey' encompassing a range of archetypal figures and situations is a very general and therefore outdated concept, and many stories do not fit into it. Some narratives, for instance, could be organized around the trickster or the self, rather than the self being the final goal of the story and the trickster being a small portion of it.

The nine archetypes form thematic clusters within narratives, which are often organized along these lines:

Life meaning

THEME 1	THEME 2	THEME 3
Social adaptation	*Reality-testing*	*Self-actualization*
Morality and rules	Parents and partners	Achievements and creativity
Two archetypes	Four archetypes	Three archetypes
the shadow	the anima	the child
the trickster	the animus	the hero
	old man/father	the self
	old woman/mother	

Theme 1: Social adaptation

This theme contains two archetypes, the shadow and the trickster, and is probably the basic one, both in human development and in narrative storytelling. Social adaptation is the first issue a human child faces as he or she enters the world. Freud talked about this issue as the problem of narcissism – the child is gradually introduced to the fact that he or she is not the only creature in the world, and has to learn to co-exist with other family members as well as society members. In other words, the child learns to 'tame' his or her narcissistic impulses. Lacan talked about the 'mirror stage' – the developmental phase when this awareness of the presence of others happens, and when the child starts to realize that he or she is one of the many individuals inhabiting the same social space. Eventually, the initial (primary) narcissism is thus replaced with a healthier version, which allows the individual to successfully co-exist with others and to see them as equal human beings with feelings and rights.

Meanwhile, society has a set of moral rules, implemented in a variety of official and unofficial codes, such as religion, law, traditions, or what is known as 'common decency'. All of them are here to make sure that the individual internalizes the ways of co-existing with others without damaging either him- or herself or others.

Jung rarely talks about narcissism *per se*, but he coined a metaphor to describe the basic, selfish impulses in human nature: the shadow (described in more detail in Chapter 2). The shadow follows us whenever we go, and our task is to integrate it, to make sense of it – otherwise it will take over us, and we will not be able to examine our negative impulses. Stories, both visual and traditional, such as Robert Louis Stevenson's *The Strange Case of Dr. Jekyll and Mr. Hyde* (1886), Oscar Wilde's *The Picture of Dorian Gray* (1890), or the more contemporary example of David Fincher's film *Fight Club* (1999), all show a male protagonist struggling to separate himself from his shadow, and to integrate its unpalatable contents (ranging from sexuality to greed and aggression) into his personality.

Interestingly enough, whereas there is an abundance of narratives about the male and his shadow, there are virtually none about women struggling with their evil *doppelgänger* – perhaps that's because, culturally, women are not allowed to be seen as anything but kind, nurturing and caring. Female characters who do not fit into this stereotype are split off into villainesses, but there is no middle ground: very few narratives portray a woman trying to make sense of her 'dark side'. Whenever this 'dark side' so much as manifests itself, like it does in Powell and Pressburger's *The Red Shoes* (1948) or Luis Buñuel *Belle de Jour* (1967), the heroine who dares to be morally ambiguous, strive for self-expression, or develop some form of agency, has to face the brutal consequences of her transgressions. The protagonist of *Red Shoes* commits suicide, while 'Belle de Jour' Séverine loses her lover and becomes a carer to her disabled husband, which effectively ends her exciting adventures as a part-time prostitute.

Only recently do we get to observe the acceptance and attempts at integrating the female shadow on television, with examples such as the BBC's *Dr. Foster* (2015–) and *Fleabag* (2016–) as well as Netflix's *Orange is the New Black* (2013–). Season 4 of Charlie Brooker's *Black Mirror* contains an episode (*Crocodile*) in which the female protagonist (played by Andrea Riseborough) is balancing her existence as a successful architect and a family woman with the life of a murderer.

Still, female shadow protagonists are fairly rare as evidently few authors consider women to be capable of going through moral struggles, or even having the capacity for moral ambivalence. Still, this is a small step in the right direction. Previously, before the VOD era, female characters and protagonists were more often than not depicted as one-dimensional – either wholly good or wholly bad, but not morally ambiguous. It is refreshing to see that digital television triggered a revolution in the way women are depicted in moving-image narratives.

The social adaptation theme precedes both maturation and self-actualization, although it is also closely linked with them. The trickster and the shadow form a continuous sliding scale that represents the issues we grapple with while trying to adapt to social norms and also trying to remain 'ourselves' – agents, independent-thinking individuals. In fact, the shadow side of the scale discusses the issue of adaptation from the point of view of society, while the trickster side examines it from the point of view of the individual agent. In other words, a story about the shadow is a story of the failure of adaptation, which is seen as an important process.

This can be expressed in a number of ways, and is closely linked to cultural specifics. For instance, Dr. Jekyll fails to absorb and deal with his aggressive side, which contrasts with the image of a decent Victorian gentle-man, and a professional at that. Similarly, the nameless protagonist of *Fight Club* (both the film and the book) does not like his role of consumer in the capitalist society. Consequently, he splits his life into a bland middle-class existence and a life of the rebel, the two never meeting in his mind. At the end of a shadow narrative, the *doppelgänger* is often killed, and the 'original' often dies with him (although some survive – usually this indicates the pres-ence of trickster motifs; that the shadow is further down the scale). A shadow narrative presents the crossing of social boundaries as a crime.

A trickster story, on the other hand, is a narrative that questions the norms of society and ascertains the power of the individual as an agent. The task of the trickster is to test the system and to find its weak points. The trickster is a metaphor for change, and is often perceived by the system as something dangerous and unpredictable, something to be framed and controlled. The trickster and the system are locked in eternal struggle, but they cannot live without each other. The crossing of boundaries in 'pure' trickster narratives is celebrated and shown as liberating because social and systemic boundaries restrain individual agency.

For instance, Jim Carrey portrayed a record number of 'pure' tricksters (unlike, say, Jack Nicholson who specializes in 'shadows' and 'shadow-tricksters'). His Lloyd Christmas in *Dumb and Dumber* (1994) fights for the right to be seen as a human being and 'to be somebody', a visible and respected member of society, albeit in a clumsy and funny way. *Ace Ventura: Pet Detective* and *Ace Ventura: When Nature Calls* (1995) mock the artificiality of civilization, while *The Mask* (1994) shows the oppressive effect of systems on the individual. The film's protagonist Stanley Ipkiss eventually learns to be himself, discovers his rights, and protects his person-ality from being encroached upon by others. A trickster narrative celebrates the crossing of social boundaries.

The middle of the scale is where the two perspectives meet, resulting in a range of trickster-shadows and shadow-tricksters. For instance, in all *Batman* narratives (including video games such as the *Arkham City* series), the Joker is a combination of the two archetypes, leaning heavily towards the shadow side of the scale. He is Batman's antagonist, but he is also the dark side of capitalism which Batman/Bruce Wayne represents. As the shadow, he reflects the capitalist's worst effects. As the trickster – and dressed in a proper trickster attire, including a clown face and bright mismatched clothes – he rejects the repressive and stifling influence of the system on the individual. The true villain of *Batman* narratives is, in fact, Bruce Wayne – a chemical and oil billionaire; the very shadowy capitalist.

Similarly, Vince Gillighan's *Breaking Bad* spinoff and prequel *Better Call Saul* (2015–) features a trickster-lawyer Saul Goodman (Bob Odenkirk)

who is 'morally flexible'. He provides advice to various high-profile crimi-
nals and, despite his highly likeable personality, is clearly an individual
belonging to 'the dark side'. In the past, he was a conman playing tricks on
strangers and scamming them of money. He enjoyed being a scammer and
a fraudster not just because this 'vocation' provided him with an income,
but also for the sheer wild creativity of it – he liked making stuff up, tell-
ing stories, and watching the victim take the bait. James (or Saul, as he
would later call himself) is offered numerous opportunities to join the system and become a professional lawyer, but always finds the demands of the
hierarchy and the strictness of the rules too constraining for his creativity.
Working at a law firm requires self-discipline, and an ability to restrain
one's impulses, all of which is too much for James (who, in a typical trickster
manner, has several other names and nicknames: James McGill and Slippin'
Jimmy). In the end, Slipping' Jimmy takes over James McGill, and he suc-
cumbs to the life outside the system (and outside the law), on the social
margins. Creativity and quick thinking, which make him a great lawyer,
also make him a great criminal.

Just like with the shadow, there are very few female tricksters in stories,
myths and moving-image narratives. A female trickster protagonist is like a
female comedian – there are few of them. However, there are many more of
them in 'gonzo' form – real-life tricksters, who have chosen protest as their
vocation. They include, to name but a few, the Russian punk band Pussy
Riot, the Ukrainian radical feminist group FEMEN, and performance artists such as Marina Abramović and Tracey Emin. All of them challenge the
established views on women and social rules.

Finally, the trickster and the shadow positions are sometimes just a matter
of perspective. When you are too ambitious, creative or original for your
social circle, and attempt to break free from it, the inhabitants of the circle
may see you as a shadow – as someone who cannot fall into line, be like
everyone else, and follow the rules. Alternatively, they can regard you as
'the foolish one' – a typical folk name for a trickster character. Yet, from
your point of view, the situation is different: you are fighting for your right
to express your creativity, for the right to be different, and to see things your
way. You are also seeking to introduce fresh new ideas and change into the
structure, for the trickster is the agent of change. You are fighting for your
agency, which is the true meaning of the trickster figure.

There follow taxonomies of the trickster and the shadow in storytelling
(examples given are far from exhaustive and are taken from a wide range of
narratives, from myth and novels to TV series). Please note that due to their
'doubling' nature, the 'social adaptation' archetypes are not always easily
separated into 'protagonists' and 'antagonists', but I have done my best.

The trickster

	Overview	Protagonist	Antagonist	Supporting character	Non-human phenomena (events, decisions, accidents, etc.)
Example		Paddington (*A Bear Called Paddington* by Michael Bond), Karlsson (*Karlsson-on-the-Roof* by Astrid Lindgren, Ace Ventura (The *Ace Ventura* films) Fletcher Reede (*Liar, Liar*, directed by Tom Shadyac Randle Patrick McMurphy (*One Flew Over the Cuckoo's Nest*, both book and film); Saul Goodman (*Better Call Saul*, created by Vince Gilligan and Peter Gould) Ivan the Fool in Russian fairy tales Wakdjunkaga (the Winnebago trickster cycle)	The Joker (*Batman*, mythology), Chip Douglas (*The Cable Guy*, directed by Ben Stiller)	The Mask (*The Mask*, directed by Chuck Russell), Drop Dead Fred (*Drop Dead Fred*, directed by Ate de Jong), Han Solo (the *Star Wars* franchise)	Carl (*Yes Man*, directed by Peyton Reed); Peter Chelsom (*Hector and the Search for Happiness*) (decisions to change life, to go travelling, to say 'yes' to new experiences, etc).

(continued)

(continued)

	Overview	Protagonist	Antagonist	Supporting character	Non-human phenomena (events, decisions, accidents, etc.)
Overall function	Balance between change and stability in a structure	Challenging a stagnant situation for the purpose of renewing the structure	• Testing the structure • Providing critique of the structure	• Helping the protagonist out of a stagnant situation for the purpose of renewal • Helping the protagonist challenge a system	• Helping the protagonist out of a stagnant situation for the purpose of renewal • Helping the protagonist challenge a system
Functions in narrative	Introduces chaos into an existing order of things	Descends on the system and triggers change (seen as a positive process – the system is 'renewed' and enriched)	Descends on the system of which the protagonist is part, and triggers change (seen as a negative process – the system 'survives')	Descends on the protagonist as a force of nature and accidentally helps him or her achieve change in a system	A decision or accident throws the protagonist out of balance and makes her or him revise the system/own life
Educational value of the narrative	Teaches to manage change	• The importance of change • The importance of revisions in the existing order • The importance of creativity • Letting go of control (anti-narcissism)	• Managing negative change • Critical attitude towards the existing system • Self-reflection which helps with the yearning for control • Integration of own narcissism	• The importance of change • The importance of revisions in the existing order • The importance of creativity • Letting go of control (anti-narcissism)	• The importance of change • The importance of revisions in the existing order • The importance of creativity • Letting go of control (anti-narcissism)

Set of attributes	• Boundary-crossing
	• Being trapped
	• The problem of the name
	• Creativity
	• No shame
	• Takes away control
	• Dissolution at the end of the narrative
	• Obsession with sex
	• Scatology
	• The animal connection

(continued)

	Overview	Protagonist	Antagonist	Supporting character	Non-human phenomena (events, decisions, accidents, etc.)
Twin archetype	The shadow The trickster forms a scale with the shadow which shows the precarious balance between narcissistic behaviour which is harmful to society, and the right to insist on one's individuality				

The trickster–shadow scale

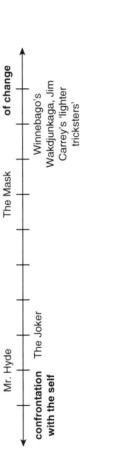

THE SHADOW

THE TRICKSTER
management
of change

Mr. Hyde   The Joker

The Mask

Winnebago's
Wakdjunkaga, Jim
Carrey's 'lighter
tricksters'

confrontation
with the self

The shadow

	Overview	Protagonist (usually as 'negative hero')	Antagonist	Supporting character	Non-human phenomena (events, decisions, accidents, general existential issues, etc.)
Example		Mr. Hyde in *Dr. Jekyll and Mr. Hyde*; Dorian Gray in *The Picture of Dorian Gray*; Walter White in *Breaking Bad* Séverine Serizy in *Belle de Jour* who is leading a double existence as a rich, bored housewife and a part-time prostitute.	The Joker (as shadow-trickster), Count Dracula in Bram Stoker's *Dracula* and its numerous adaptations	Lord Henry Wotton in *The Picture of Dorian Gray*	Crime, human cruelty and the unjust system in *Breaking Bad*; Crime and human cruelty in *Fargo* (TV version), created by Noah Hawley
Overall function	Shows the inevitability and objectivity of the instinctual side of both nature and human nature	Explores the narcissistic and instinctual side of human nature in social settings	Explores the narcissistic and instinctual side of human nature in social settings	Explores the narcissistic and instinctual side of human nature in social settings	Explores the narcissistic and instinctual side of human nature in social settings

Functions in narrative	Explores the possibility of integration of the instinctive and narcissistic impulses into human behaviour	• Shows the existence of the narcissistic traits in human nature. • Shows the dangers of not integrating antisocial impulses	• Shows the existence of the narcissistic traits in human nature • Shows the dangers of not integrating antisocial impulses	• Shows the existence of evil as an inevitable phenomenon, which is also part of human nature
Educational value of the narrative	Challenges idealistic vision of the world	Teaches to integrate the selfish and undesirable traits of human nature; shows their dangers if they are left split off	Teaches to integrate the selfish and undesirable traits of human nature; shows their dangers if they are left split off	The 'existential' moment: the objective existence of evil; also as an inevitable part of human nature

(continued)

(continued)

	Overview	Protagonist (usually as 'negative hero')	Antagonist	Supporting character	Non-human phenomena (events, decisions, accidents, general existential issues, etc.)
Set of attributes		• A character that harbours evil intentions (or intentions incompatible with a civilized society), but splits them off into a separate personality • The protagonist often challenges his or her split personality, and dies with it	• A character representing the negative, selfish traits (sometimes projected on to by other characters) • Is conquered by the protagonist or another representative of the moral system	• A secondary character who is morally ambiguous; may attempt to spread the corruption	Unexplained existence of evil in the world that has to be accepted
Twin archetypes	The trickster				

Theme 2: Reality-testing

This theme comprises four archetypes, each of which also has a significant negative aspect. If the trickster and the shadow bounce off each other, the anima, the animus, the old man (father) and the old woman (mother) have their own negative aspects to bounce off in narratives.

Out of the four, the parental figures represent the past of the protagonist, and the anima and the animus her or his future. This set of archetypes outlines sexual development and discovery of romantic attraction, emergence of responsibility for others as well as appropriation of tradition. This is a 'communal', tribal set of archetypes dealing with family and community ties which usually show the passing of cultural legacy from one generation to the next, while at the same time renewing and strengthening this legacy. As metaphors, the four archetypes also manage human ability to tell the difference between the real person and the imaginary object: the father or mother as a complex individual rather than an idealized image; and also a romantic partner as a real person rather than a fantasy. In other words, these are the archetypes of 'reality-testing'. The combination of positive and negative traits in these archetypes are a big part of their 'reality-testing' aspects.

In their positive version, the parental archetypes are often presented in narratives as caring and helpful, carrying the protagonist through difficulties or giving him or her useful advice. For instance, in Russian fairy tales, 'the father' often appears in the form of an animal (wolf, bear) and gives timely advice to the male protagonist who is lost in the woods. In the Russian fairy tale called 'Morozko', a female protagonist is saved by Father Frost just when she is about to freeze in the winter forest. A 'good mother' often appears as an elderly figure or a beautiful young mother, but she is always selfless and prepared to sacrifice herself for the sake of her children. The 'good' parents' helpfulness is also presented in narratives as moral when, in fact, it is an evolutionary trait and has to be seen as such. The same goes for cooperation – another subject that is often present in Theme 2. The hero is still reliant on his parents for knowledge and wisdom, and is gradually learning to explore the world on his or her own. Everything we think are moral, definitively human traits – parental self-sacrifice, hard work, cooperation – are actually evolutionary, animal traits. There is nothing purely human in human behaviour. Only the rationalization of lower traits as higher traits is perhaps something that we added to this mix. Society tends to rationalize desirable behaviour as 'moral' and undesirable behaviour as 'immoral' when, in fact, both can be perfectly natural in the animal world.

The 'bad' parents, on the other hand, are often presented in narratives in black-and-white terms as demonic and inhuman. The witch, Baba Yaga, the cruel stepmother, a neglectful mother shown as wanting to engulf the protagonist, or even all other characters. Similarly, evil wizards or brutal fathers destroy and objectify their children. The protagonist is intimidated by them and is struggling to survive on their own.

The more thoughtful narratives present 'bad parents' as perhaps individuals grappling with a whole range of problems of their own, and objectifying their children as a result. For instance, Merida from the Pixar/ Disney animation *Brave* (2012) has a mother who expects her daughter to be a meek princess who needs to get married and start a family, when Merida herself loves adventures and wants to be a hero. The daughter ends up using a spell which transforms the mother into a bear, and then deals with the beast that her mother metaphorically is to her. The mother is not shown in the film as entirely negative – only as steeped in tradition and prejudice. Yet, to Merida, she is the problem which prevents the princess from achieving her full potential.

One of the issues Theme 2 raises is the treatment of parents as individuals rather than expecting self-sacrifice from them in all cases without exception. 'The reality test' shows the protagonist the boundary between dependence on the parents and the start of independent life.

Moreover, the mother forms a sliding scale with the anima, and the father with the animus. In this sense, people looking for a partner of whatever (not necessarily opposite) sex model this partner first of all on a parent. The Freudians and Lacan famously had a lot to say on the issue, and so did theorists like John Bowlby, but discussing the intricacies of psychological dependency is beyond the point of this chapter. Let us just say that this Jungian version of the Oedipus complex (it is hoped) does not contain the pathologizing undertones of its Freudian counterpart. In this sense, it is normal to have characters whose choice of partners is clearly traceable to their parents. The best example of this is perhaps Andrej Tarkovsky's *The Mirror* (1975), in which the protagonist's mother and his wife are played by the same actress, Margarita Terekhova.

The mother/old wise woman

	Overview	Protagonist	Antagonist or negative protagonist	Supporting character (positive or negative)	Non-human phenomena (memories of childhood, visions, fantasies, dreams, metaphors, other representations of the maternal instinct)
Example		Famously, *Dr Who* which presented its first female Doctor in Series 11, released in 2018 *Places in the Heart; Terms of Endearment*	The numerous neglectful mothers in Netflix's *Orange is the New Black; Brave; Sleeping Beauty; Frozen; Snow Queen*	*Psycho;* Tarkovsky's *The Mirror; The Terminator;* Murderers' mothers in Netflix's *Mindhunter; Mother!*	Documentaries such as *Planet Earth* and *Blue Planet*
Overall function	Nurture, care, protect, inspire and support; 'create' the individual	Shows bravery and devotion, protecting the children from danger, often risking her own life	Does not perform her duties of the mother well, endangering the protagonist or the character	• Care for the protagonist (positive); neglect of the protagonist (negative) • Demands respect for the mother, and her sacrifice	Respect for Mother Earth; showing abuse of Mother Earth; ecological issues

(continued)

(continued)

	Overview	Protagonist	Antagonist or negative protagonist	Supporting character (positive or negative)	Non-human phenomena (memories of childhood, visions, fantasies, dreams, metaphors, other representations of the maternal instinct)
Functions in narrative	• Protecting the children, caring for the children • Unconditional love, the power of love, the power of maternal • Knowledge and wisdom • Teaching to respect the maternal	Protects and inspires her children	• Neglects or actively attempts to destroy the children or the protagonist • Demands respect for herself and her sacrifice • Demands respect for the order established by her	• Positive: offers protection, help or inspiration to the protagonist • Negative: neglects or actively attempts to destroy the protagonist	Asks for respect for the maternal principle
Educational value of the narrative	Teaches respect for the mother, her power and her sacrifice	Teaches respect for the mother, her power and her sacrifice	Teaches respect for the power of the maternal/Mother Earth	Teaches respect for the mother, her power and her sacrifice	Teaches respect for the power of the maternal/Mother Earth

Set of attributes	Creative:
	- Caring
	- Nurturing
	- Inspiring (a source of creativity)
	- Protecting
	- Offering unconditional love
	Destructive:
	- Neglectful
	- Angry
	- Selfish
	- Is fallible or too human
	- Goddess of Death
Twin archetype	The anima

The mother–anima scale

The Mother

Maternal figure

Romantic partner based on the maternal figure

The Anima

Romantic partner

The father/old wise man

	Overview	Protagonist	Antagonist	Supporting character	Non-human phenomena (events, decisions, accidents, etc.)
Example	Dr. Who		Lord Voldemort (*Harry Potter*), Darth Vader (*Star Wars*)	Obi Wan, Yoda in *Star Wars*; the Satan in *The Master and Margarita*	
Overall function		Help and provision of knowledge to the protagonist	A keeper of secret knowledge or powerful device which can destroy the world	Help and provision of knowledge to the protagonist	
Functions in narrative		Shows wisdom and knowledge in overcoming obstacles; provides advice	Provides negative inspiration for the protagonist for overcoming obstacles	Shows wisdom and knowledge in overcoming obstacles; provides advice	
Educational value of the narrative		Helps find the meaning of existence	Helps find the meaning of existence	Helps find the meaning of existence	
Set of attributes		• Wisdom • Keeper of knowledge • Powerful • Protector	• Keeper of knowledge • Powerful • Destructive • Leader	• Wisdom • Keeper of knowledge • Powerful • Protector	
Twin archetypes	The animus				

The father–animus scale

The anima and the animus are traditionally presented as opposites, performing different functions for people who experience them. The anima is the impossible combination of angelic and seductive/dangerous traits, forever split, forever switching between the two. A dangerous siren or a princess waiting to be saved from a tower by her hero on a white horse, the anima is the ultimate seat of male projections. By contrast, the animus is the 'talkative male', sometimes several, in a woman's head (see more on this in the previous chapter). Compared to the mostly silent anima, the animus is allowed to speak. Conservative Jungians also could not envisage a woman having an anima, or a man an animus. For them, it was all a matter of heteronormative opposites.

This book does not follow this traditional Jungian vision. Anima and animus are shown as equal, and performing practically the same function: they remind the individual of her or his independence from the parents; and in folklore and authored fairy tales, it is often the act of searching for them that makes the hero mature. For instance (and I am deliberately using a narrative with a female protagonist), in *The Snow Queen*, a tale by Hans Christian Andersen, the girl Gerda risks her life to find her friend Kai, who was bewitched and stolen by the cold and heartless Snow Queen. After many adventures, the girl finds the Snow Queen's ice palace and melts the splinter of the ice mirror in Kai's eye, which was preventing the boy from experiencing emotions and enjoying the real world. Apart from the obvious metaphor of weaning a partner off his mother, taking him away from fantasy and making him see reality, the fairy tale contains a strong and persistent female protagonist willing to fight for her partner as well as separating him from her animus.

The animus-father and anima-mother scale indicate a degree of maturity, acceptance of reality and ability to separate real people from fantasies. It is also interesting that often the anima and the animus have the voice (manifested as the acts of singing or speaking) as one of their main features. Although the anima does not often speak, she is 'allowed' to sing as an act of seduction (like the sirens or the beautiful cabaret performers of the Golden Age of Hollywood). This is probably the metaphor for the 'mating call', which points to the principal function of the two archetypes.

Another interesting feature is that in folklore they often start off as animals (this trend is replicated by contemporary narratives) – a frog, a hairy beast, a bear – but are eventually allowed to become human. This stands for the 'reality-testing' moment of the narrative: overcoming the fear of the other not as a fantasy person or a duplicate parent, but as a real one; accepting the partner as an individual.

History of cinema abides in numerous animas, seductive and dangerous, beautiful and angelic, and mostly dependent on men. As protagonists, antagonists and supporting characters, anima characters have been relying on being saved and validated by their male 'heroes'. Perhaps a time will come for a more realistic portrayal of anima characters, for they are rarely lucky enough to be treated as 'real' by the male protagonists who win them over or obtain them as a mate.

The animus is usually presented as an antagonist or a supporting character. A protagonist animus is very rare, much like the protagonist anima, mainly because the 'finding the partner' narrative type focuses on the actions of the person looking for a partner rather than the potential romantic object.

Up until relatively recently, the animus narrative was the main type of story available to a female protagonist. A female character (obligatorily beautiful) would be cast as searching for an ideal husband or a partner who would take care of her and the future family. This potential partner would be made to go through various tests in order to ascertain his suitability for the role. A female protagonist was perpetually and exclusively looking for love, with very few interests outside this narrow focus (Marilyn Monroe's characters epitomize this approach).

The view of the female role in narratives was supported by such stalwarts of narratology as Joseph Campbell, so it is not surprising that the film industry has been replicating this view for decades. Apparently, Campbell thought that a woman does not need to explore the world as she is 'already there', already perfect – unlike the male hero. The psychotherapist Maureen Murdock was interested in Campbell's views on the female journey, and his response was rather blunt:

> I wanted to hear Campbell's views. I was surprised when he responded that women don't need to make the journey. 'In the whole mythological tradition the woman is there. All she has to do is to realize that she's the place that people are trying to get to. When a woman realizes what her wonderful character is, she's not going to get messed up with the notion of being pseudo-male.'
>
> (Murdock, 2013: 7)

More recently, Hollywood was forced to follow in the footsteps of VOD television (as well as Scandinavian genre drama such as *The Killing* (2007–2012) and *The Bridge* (2011–)) and introduce female characters whose primary aim was not to find love, and who had other pursuits such as moral issues or self-actualization. Finally, the female protagonist was allowed to go outside Theme 2 and explore other avenues apart from love and family. In other words, the woman character's opportunity to go on a journey, or many journeys, that are not about finding a guy to settle with has improved significantly. At last, we have female detectives, soldiers, doctors and other characters whose aims on the journey are not limited to being beautiful and waiting for a prince or to become a mother. Even large franchises such as *Star Wars* now have female fighters and even a female Jedi (Rey, played by Daisy Ridley).

The anima

	Overview	Protagonist	Antagonist	Supporting character	Non-human phenomena (events, decisions, accidents, etc.)
Example		Pretty much every role played by Marilyn Monroe; Gilda in *Gilda* (directed by	Lola Lola in *The Blue Angel* (1930) (directed by Josef von Stenberg; female Bond villains	Princess Leia in the *Star Wars* franchise	Nature, weather and motherland in Tarkovsky's *The Mirror* (1975)
Overall function	Reality-testing	Explores: Finding a romantic connection, sexual love, finding a partner	Explores: Fear of sexuality, of sexual love; fear of growing up, awareness of the dangers of adult life	Explores: Finding a romantic connection, sexual love, finding a partner.	Provides inspiration and creativity
Functions in narrative		Explores: • Finding a romantic connection, sexual love, finding a partner • Winning over a partner • The boundary between the fantasy object and the real person (fantasy vs reality)	Explores: • Fear of reality, of maturity of growing up • The contrast between fantasy and reality • Fear of sexuality, of sexual love	Explores: • Finding a romantic connection, sexual love, finding a partner • Winning over a partner • The boundary between the fantasy object and the real person (fantasy vs reality)	

(continued)

(continued)

	Overview	Protagonist	Antagonist	Supporting character	Non-human phenomena (events, decisions, accidents, etc.)
Educational value of the narrative	Initiation into adult life; • learning to find a partner, • learning to distinguish between the object and reality, • learning to distinguish between suitable and unsuitable partners	Initiation into adult life; • learning to find a partner, • learning to distinguish between the object and reality, • learning to distinguish between suitable and unsuitable partners	Initiation into adult life; • learning to find a partner, • learning to distinguish between the object and reality, • learning to distinguish between suitable and unsuitable partners	Initiation into adult life; • learning to find a partner, • learning to distinguish between the object and reality, • learning to distinguish between suitable and unsuitable partners	Initiation into adult life; • learning to find a partner, • learning to distinguish between the object and reality, • learning to distinguish between suitable and unsuitable partners

Set of attributes			
• Motivating/ inspiring • Beautiful • Represented metonymically by the voice • Speaking to the soul • Evasive, clashing with reality • Exhilarating • Seductive, brings sexual awakening • Has to be fought for/won over	• Aggressive and dangerous • Represented by an animal • Oversexed • Controlling, overbearing • Capricious, demanding, unpredictable	• Motivating/ inspiring • Beautiful • Represented metonymically by the voice • Speaking to the soul • Evasive, clashing with reality • Exhilarating • Triggers sexual awakening	• Motivating/ inspiring • Beautiful • Represented metonymically by the voice • Speaking to the soul • Evasive, clashing with reality • Exhilarating • Triggers sexual awakening
Twin archetypes	The mother/old wise woman		

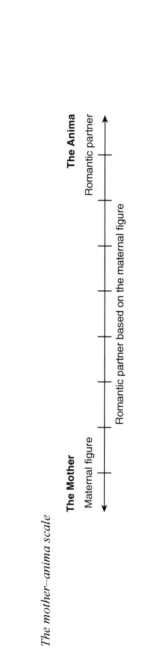

The mother–anima scale

The Mother
Maternal figure

Romantic partner based on the maternal figure

The Anima
Romantic partner

The animus

	Overview	Protagonist	Antagonist	Supporting character	Non-human phenomena (events, decisions, etc.)
Example		Kai in Hans Christian Andersen's fairy tale *The Snow Queen*; Adam in *Only Lovers Left Alive* (2013)	The Beast in *Beauty and the Beast*; Count Bluebeard in *Bluebeard*; The Wolf in *Little Red Riding Hood*; Dick in Jill Soloway's *I Love Dick* (both the book and the Amazon TV series); Edward Cullen in *Twilight* (2008) (Catherine Hardwicke, Chris Weitz); Bill Compton (*True Blood*); Boris Lermontov in *Red Shoes*	Nino in *Amelie* (2001); Joe's lovers in Lars von Trier's *Nymphomaniac* (2013); *Bridget Jones* films; Julian Craster in *Red Shoes* (1948) (directed by Michael Powell and Emeric Pressburger)	

(continued)

(continued)

	Overview	Protagonist	Antagonist	Supporting character	Non-human phenomena (events, decisions, accidents, etc.)
Overall function	Reality-testing	Explores: Finding a romantic connection, sexual love, finding a partner	Explores: Fear of sexuality, of sexual love; fear of growing up, awareness of the dangers of adult life	Explores: Finding a romantic connection, sexual love, finding a partner	Provides inspiration and creativity
Functions in narrative		Explores: • Finding a romantic connection, sexual love, finding a partner • Winning over a partner • The boundary between the fantasy object and the real person (fantasy vs reality)	Explores: • Fear of reality, of maturity of growing up • The contrast between fantasy and reality • Fear of sexuality, of sexual love	Explores: • Finding a romantic connection, sexual love, finding a partner • Winning over a partner • The boundary between the fantasy object and the real person (fantasy vs reality)	

Educational value of the narrative	Initiation into adult life; learning to find a partner, learning to distinguish between the object and reality, learning to distinguish between suitable and unsuitable partners	Initiation into adult life; learning to find a partner, learning to distinguish between the object and reality, learning to distinguish between suitable and unsuitable partners	Initiation into adult life; learning to find a partner, learning to distinguish between the object and reality, learning to distinguish between suitable and unsuitable partners	Initiation into adult life; learning to find a partner, learning to distinguish between the object and reality, learning to distinguish between suitable and unsuitable partners	Initiation into adult life; learning to find a partner, learning to distinguish between the object and reality, learning to distinguish between suitable and unsuitable partners
Set of attributes		• Motivating/inspiring • Beautiful • Represented metonymically by the voice • Speaking to the soul • Evasive, clashing with reality • Exhilarating • Seductive, brings sexual awakening • Has to be fought for/won over	• Aggressive and dangerous • Represented by an animal • Oversexed • Controlling, overbearing • Capricious, demanding, unpredictable	• Motivating/inspiring • Beautiful • Represented metonymically by the voice • Speaking to the soul • Evasive, clashing with reality • Exhilarating • Triggers sexual awakening	• Motivating/inspiring • Beautiful • Represented metonymically by the voice • Speaking to the soul • Evasive, clashing with reality • Exhilarating • Triggers sexual awakening
Twin archetypes	The father/old wise man				

The animus–father scale

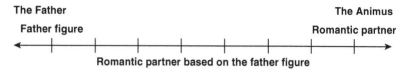

The Father   The Animus

Father figure   Romantic partner

Romantic partner based on the father figure

Theme 3: Self-actualization

Overall, this theme covers the conflict of free will versus God's omniscience and control, and contains three archetypes: the child, the hero and the self. Additionally, Theme 3 touches upon the inspiration and motivation behind the impulse to self-actualize, to find yourself, and to individuate. The 'free will versus control' conflict is not necessarily presented in Theme 3 narratives as a form of rebellion against God; often it is about exploring the balance between the two, or examining the dual nature of God (helpful versus destructive). Omniscience is one of its key features.

The self in Theme 3 narratives does not necessarily take the shape of a human god but it dominates the theme, and in a way all three themes. Jung points out in his essays about the so-called UFO phenomena that, in the middle of the twentieth century, 'the mysteries of god' trope became more technogenic in its expressions, often taking the shape of alien arrival and abduction stories (see more about this in Chapter 2). Many contemporary narratives exploring the issue of free will versus god's will end up discussing god in its newest forms – god as an alien and god as technology. In fact, the sci-fi genre was born simultaneously with the contemporary versions of the self: aliens, technology and artificial intelligence. The latter was already being explored in Romantic fiction, which started the dialogue about the dangers of industrialization and technology, for instance in Mary Shelley's *Frankenstein* (the monster) and E. T. A. Hoffman's *The Sandman* (Olympia).

Although the self has acquired new shapes, deep down this is still the same archetype. Or, to use proper Jungian terminology, the archetype of the self now has a new range of archetypal images that are more in line with the realities of industrial and post-industrial societies. The god portrayed is still the same complex archetype of the self – omniscient, conflicting, controversial, elusive and full of riddles. It speaks a strange language, which human beings have to learn, or at the very least decipher. Sometimes it is inexplicably silent. It gives human beings riddles and puzzles which they have to solve; sometimes it provides advice, and at other times it completely throws people off balance. This is not a kind, benevolent god, but a tough one; the god that makes you work hard and sometimes suffer; the self in all its manifestations is the metaphor for how demanding and punishing the individuation process can be.

Different media present different sides of the self. This concerns all kinds of sci-fi lore, including aliens and artificial intelligence. For instance, in *Arrival* (2016, directed by Denis Villeneuve), the self is presented as an alien looking like a giant octopus. Louise (Amy Adams) is a linguist who is hired to learn the language of the heptapod guests, which leads to the discovery that the aliens had come to Earth to spread the message of unity and peace. Similarly, *E.T., the Extra-Terrestrial* (1982) depicts extra-terrestrial guests as benevolent and even cute.

Narratives with 'the good self', however, are outnumbered by warnings about its potentially destructive side. Films such as *Mars Attacks!* (1996), *The Day the Earth Stood Still* (1951), *Independence Day* (1996) and its sequel, and numerous other mass invasion movies warn the viewers of the power and unpredictability of god-like forces – of the dangers of the self. In video gaming, the self often emerges in puzzle games in which the player is given little information about the circumstances in which they find themselves, and attempts to decipher the ways of this foreign world. Examples of this include, for instance, *Portal* (Valve) and *The Talos Principle* (Croteam). Some of the manifestations of the self in film and television are less obvious and remain vague, for instance Andrej Tarkovsky's *Stalker* (1979) and *Solaris* (1982).

Movies such as *Blade Runner* (1982) and *Blade Runner 2049* (2017), the *Terminator* and the *Matrix* franchises depict the self as a relentless and unstoppable god of technology which is a threat to humans. VOD television has also been capitalizing on the negative side of the archetype of the self. It pays special attention to the subject of artificial intelligence and the possibility that it will take over the world. To name but a few, Netflix has *Black Mirror* and *AI: Artificial Intelligence*; Amazon has *Humans* (2015–) and HBO has *Westworld*. Some of them are particularly scathing and negative in their observation of humankind and its relationship with the self/ god figure. For instance, Charlie Brooker's *Black Mirror* (2017) contains vignettes about the future of humanity in the world progressively dominated by computers. All of them show human beings as being undermined by technology (*Fifteen Million Merits* (S1), *Crocodile*, *Metalhead* (S4), which is a re-making of the Terminator idea), while others show people as being too lazy to make their own mistakes – that is, too lazy to individuate, relying on the predictive precision of their god instead (*Hang the DJ* (S4), *Nosedive* (S3), *The Waldo Moment* (S2)).

All of these narratives explore the issue of free will: do we make life decisions ourselves or are we led by a larger force on our individuation path; an omniscient force that controls us? Isn't technology a better god than the previous god? In the past, people were asking deities about weather patterns, love, luck, and everything else. Their predictions worked, at best, in half of all cases. Now we have weather forecasts delivered to our mobiles, predictive dating apps, and everything else predictive. Technology leaves a small margin for human error. This is an excellent god. But is this the one we wanted?

The child and the hero

The child, the hero and the self form a continuous line that represents personal development. The child is at the start of the line, standing for the beginning of human motivation and self-actualization. The hero is its continuation, and almost always occupies the role of the protagonist. The self is the (unachievable) goal of the individuation process which, nevertheless, serves as a sort of 'light at the end of the tunnel, spurring the hero on'.

The archetype of the child itself stands for motivation and creativity, and often emerges as a secondary character or a memory at the moment when the hero protagonist is stuck or has run out of steam. The child is pure and naïve, untouched by the corrupting influence of society, and it is a source of spiritual renewal. Some directors, for instance Tim Burton, build their imagery around the child archetype. The majority of Tim Burton's protagonists are either children or stuck in the childhood mode, which keeps alive their creativity and individuality. The hero is the one who searches for the true self. She or he is characterized by her or his ability to be motivated, brave, decisive and to overcome obstacles. Contemporary mythology likes to present them as schematic, but the searching hero character can also possess a lot of depth.

Up until twenty years ago, the hero archetype both in fiction and in moving-image narratives had been predominantly male, while female characters had been stuck in the supporting roles of the 'beautiful anima' or 'the doting mother'. The very few female protagonists were mainly allowed Theme 2 quests, namely the quest for a partner (Monroe in *Gentlemen Prefer Blondes*). More recently, the fight has been to steer the very few women's protagonist roles from those of the hunter for a perfect partner (the animus) towards the hero, the old wise person (like Jodie Whittaker's *Dr. Who*), the shadow – or, in fact, anything else but the role of the sexual object or of someone searching for a perfect man. Characters such as Rey in the *Star Wars* franchise, *Wonder Woman* (2017) and numerous TV shows (such as Netflix's *Jessica Jones*) continue to challenge the heteronormative approach of classical Hollywood.

It has also been a struggle to challenge archetypal representations of female sexuality, namely of the female as a passive object interested in prominent males. Shows such as Netflix's *Orange Is the New Black* (2013–) draw its female characters (not just the protagonist's) sexual interest away from exclusively 'the animus', while Amazon's *I Love Dick* (2016) protagonist aggressively pursues her male target, not stopping at anything.

The situation with gender representation among characters belonging to the child topos is similar to that of the hero or the self. The child is a future hero, and narratives involving this topos often map out this future with its hopes and dreams. Traditionally, authors and screenwriters have not been particularly interested in the girl-hero future. However, things have recently been looking up. A far cry from only an occasional female child protagonist, such as Alice or Dorothy in *fin de siècle* novels, girls in today's narratives do not have to wear dresses or look feminine; they have super-power abilities (Eleven in *Stranger Things*), are good at maths (Mary Adler in *Gifted*, 2017) and in training to be knights (Arya Stark in HBO's *Game of Thrones*). At last, there is some kind of variety on offer for the female child as the future hero.

The self

	Overview	Protagonist	Antagonist
Example		*The Last Temptation of Christ; The Passion of Christ*	*Arrival; The Talos Principle; Mars Attacks!; War of the Worlds*
Overall function	• Deferral of responsibility for the individuation process • Providing motivation for self-reflection and self-development	Named character whose task is to lead the people towards self-realization and providing self-reflection	An unfathomable force (for example, aliens or AI) leading 'the people' towards self-realization and providing self-reflection
Functions in narrative	Leads the protagonist or society on a journey by providing them with clues and puzzles	Attempts to show a glimpse of truth to society	• Overwhelms society with the desire to find the truth • Behaves in a manipulative manner • Attacks the society and prompts it to defend its values

Educational value of the narrative	Finding motivation for actualization	Providing motivation for self-actualization	Providing motivation for self-actualization

Set of attributes	• Unfathomable
	• Unpredictable
	• Morally ambiguous: neither good nor bad
	• Exposing communication gaps (speaks an unknown language that needs to be learned)
	• Overwhelming
	• Guidance:
	  a Leaving puzzles (less forceful versions),
	  b giving instructions or
	  c commands (more forceful versions).		

Twin archetype	The child		

The Child ←———|———|———|———|———|———|———|———|———→ The Self

The child

	Overview	Protagonist	Antagonist or negative protagonist	Supporting character	Non-human phenomena (memories of childhood, visions, fantasies, dreams, etc.)
Example		Edward Scissorhands; Charlie and the Chocolate Factory; Stranger Things	Child's Play; Exorcist	Dolly Dearest	The Mirror
Overall function	Nostalgia about pre-systemic (before matu|rity) creativity and purity	Takes back to the 'before the dawn of the system' time when everything was full of awe and creativity	• Plays with the fear of losing creativity to maturation • Plays with the vulnerability of creative states Shows the importance of systems and the dangers of uncontrolled creativity	• Helps the protagonist regain creativity and a sense of being alive (positive) • Warns of maturity ahead (negative)	• Helps the protagonist regain creativity and a sense of being alive (positive) • Warns of maturity ahead (negative)
Functions in narrative	Helps a character regain their lost drive/ inspiration	Helps a character to regain inspiration to complete a task		Helps a character to regain inspiration to complete a task	Helps a character to regain inspiration to complete a task

Educational value of the narrative	• The quest for creativity and the sensation of 'being alive' • Solving the dichotomy between growing up and remaining open-minded	Keeping alive the sense of awe and wonder which are instrumental in personal progression	Warning about the dichotomy between: • A sense of vulnerability that comes with creativity • The rigidity of adulthood	Keeping alive the sense of awe and wonder which are instrumental in self-development	Keeping alive the sense of awe and wonder which are instrumental in self-development
Set of attributes	• Creativity • Purity, naivety • Lack of understanding of the adult world • Nostalgia for the past, for the lost youth • 'The drive', the sense of being alive, of feeling acutely • Being special, being chosen, being unique • Being born of the two worlds, having a twin set of parents: the real and the celestial				
Twin archetype	The hero				

The hero

	Overview	Protagonist	Antagonist	Supporting character	Non-human phenomena (events, decisions, accidents, etc.)
Example		Luke Skywalker and Rey in *Star Wars*, all renditions of Batman, Superman, Superwoman, Superman, Spiderman, Catwoman, G.I. Jane, etc.	N/A	The Avengers	N/A
Overall function	Searching for oneself	• Explores resilience and shows the process of overcoming obstacles in life		• Explores resilience and shows the process of overcoming obstacles in life	
Functions in narrative	Searching for oneself	• Provides a canvas for examples of overcoming the obstacles		• Provides a canvas for examples of overcoming the obstacles	

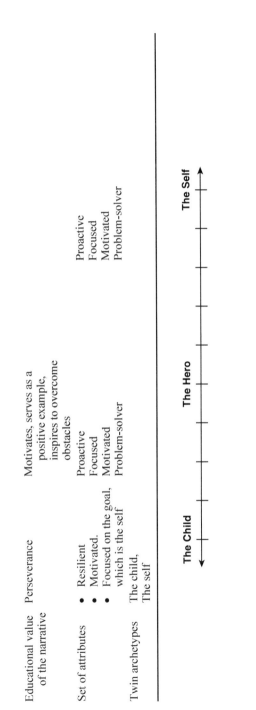

Educational value of the narrative	Perseverance	Motivates, serves as a positive example, inspires to overcome obstacles	
Set of attributes	• Resilient • Motivated. • Focused on the goal, which is the self	Proactive Focused Motivated Problem-solver	Proactive Focused Motivated Problem-solver
Twin archetypes	The child, The self		

The Child — The Hero — The Self

The hierarchy of themes in narratives

Narratives are rarely built around a single archetype or a theme (although this is possible with smaller forms such as a short story or a stand-alone episode), and often combine a range of them, culminating in a complex hierarchy of subjects.

For instance, there are overlaps between Themes 1 (social adaptation) and 2 (reality-testing). The two are shown together, for instance, in *Bildungsroman*-style narratives (for instance, *Twilight* or *Stranger Things*) when a young protagonist finds himself or herself in a new place (such as a school or a university), and is forced to both adapt to the complex new environment (dealing with change, going through liminal time – the trickster subject) while also dealing with the issue of romantic and sexual attraction.

Combined, Themes 1 (social adaptation) and 3 (self-actualization) often result in the themes of 'playing god' and 'controlling the double'. Narratives such as *I, Robot* (2004), the *Blade Runner* franchise, and the HBO series *Westworld* explore the possibility of humanoid robots rebelling against their human masters. A twister version of this combination also appears in 'Metalhead' (*Black Mirror*, S4), in which a terminator-like robodog relentlessly pursues its human targets and eventually outsmarts even the most resilient and resourceful of survivors. Another S4 *Black Mirror* vignette, 'USS Callister', features replicated human beings trapped inside a video game while their master (Jesse Plemons) exercises complete control over them, including torture.

The merger of Themes 2 and 3 often results in 'creating a partner' motif; for instance, when the protagonist plays god and invents a 'perfect partner' (George Bernard Shaw's *Pygmalion*, as *My Fair Lady* (1964), *Her* (2013), *Ex Machina* (2015)) or when protagonists are 'fated' to find each other ('Hang the DJ', *Black Mirror*, S4).

Finally, complex narratives often comprise all nine archetypes, arranged as different strands or as different issues the protagonist is solving, in no particular order.

4   The ego, the persona and the self
The conflict

The individuation process with its archetypes is linked to the personality dynamic. What does a character's personality consist of? How do they handle various impulses within themselves, how do they keep the balance between the demands of society and personal interests? Do they show their true self to the world, or do they develop an inscrutable mask to protect their vulnerabilities? Finally, how do they handle the issue of the meaning of life and the question of free will? Jung's answer to this was to picture the personality as a sort of cake with layers, the main ones being the ego, the persona and the self.

Human personality, according to Jung, is complex. It does not simply consist of the conscious 'you' who wakes up in the morning, drags your body out of bed, and makes a cup of coffee in order to be able to face reality and to keep up with ever-changing life circumstances. This 'you' was called by Jung 'ego-consciousness'. It is close to what we call 'identity' – this is my self, the real 'me', how I feel it, how I define myself, who I see when I look in the mirror.

This 'me' is attached to reality and responds to its demands and pressures. It makes decisions, puts signatures on documents, testifies in court, sits exams, observes deadlines, pays bills, makes phone calls, interacts with clients at work, and does a myriad of other duties which require being diligent and responsible, being aware of external reality, and understanding the boundaries between people. We ordinarily assume that all these actions are fully conscious, and that they stem from our solid personality centre.

However, our personality also comprises other elements. One of them is the mask which we put on every day and which reflects society's vision of who we are: a mother, a wife, an employee, a boss, a teacher, an artist, etc. The mask sometimes takes control of us, we forget who we really are, and lock ourselves in these external roles, forgetting to scrutinize and question them. In Analytical Psychology, this mask, which is closely linked to social status, is called 'the persona'.

Our existence is plagued, on the one hand, by the constant struggle with the unconscious, and, on the other, by the necessity to manage societal expectations. Our ultimate aim in life is to solve these inner and outer conflicts, and to establish an emotional balance that would protect us from worry, conflict and pain. This psychological state of peace and happiness Jung called 'the self'. He and other Jungian theorists repeatedly emphasized that it is impossible to achieve this psychological condition, but that the mere dream of finally coming to peace with ourselves and our society is what drives us on the difficult and bumpy journey of self-discovery.

Ego-consciousness

Monday morning, 8 a.m. You have had your breakfast, left the house, and are on your way to work. The walk takes about 15 minutes, and is quite pleasant, save for a busy crossing on which you have to wait. En route you are admiring the muted sunlight seeping through the thin layer of clouds, the dry leaves carried by the wind, the magnificent trees wearing multi-coloured dresses . . . Then you reach the pedestrian crossing. It is quite busy, and there are at least ten people waiting to cross the road. The flow of cars seems endless. Suddenly, you feel annoyed, both at the crowd and the cars. You can smell the fumes. The people are standing too close to each other. A man accidentally touches you with his backpack, and apologizes. You very nearly tell him to be careful with his bag, but restrain yourself. Eventually the green light flashes, and you feel relieved.

Finally, you enter the office building. You look around in case your boss is nearby and you need to say 'hello'. He is not, but you notice a colleague in the corner who is talking to another colleague. You think she has noticed you, but pretended not to. You feel slighted. Annoyed, you open your email, expecting to see a deluge of complaints and demands for help. Yet, the very first email you read is a 'thank you' letter from a grateful customer who appreciates you being so calm and professional in difficult circumstances. Your balance is restored. Now you feel appreciated again, and ready to face the next challenge.

This little story is meant to show the complexity of the dynamic between consciousness and the unconscious. Jung writes that the ego is the centre of the conscious mind (CW 7: para. 365). Your ego guides you through the long list of daily tasks, from waking up and brushing your teeth to switching on the computer. We feel as if we are in control of our actions; we are always totally responsible for everything we do. After all, we choose to wait for the green light before crossing the street instead of rushing ahead and risking being hit by a bus. We are also fully conscious when we greet our colleagues or when we are writing an email.

Yet, Jung notes, the centre of consciousness is not the exclusive owner of our daily actions: 'the ego-conscious personality is only a part of the whole man, and its life does not represent the total life' (CW 7: para. 244). This is because consciousness is relative, and 'its contents are conscious and unconscious at the same time' (CW 8: para. 397). Although we (or rather, our ego) tend to think that we are fully aware of reality at all times, the unconscious psyche is not a 'subliminal appendix to the conscious mind' (CW 8: para. 373). Jung even hypothesized that, alarmingly, the unconscious may be autonomous to such an extent that it possesses its own 'ego' and contains all functions of human consciousness (CW 8: para. 369). This is a scary thought! Imagine a world inside you, a sort of a living ocean with responses of its own, somewhat like Stanisław Lem's Solaris from the 1961 novel of the same name. This ocean is capable of making decisions and guiding your reactions to the outside stimuli. In principle, this means that there are numerous other drives and processes underneath the surface of the water, and our walk to work is influenced by them.

At the start of your journey to work, you were breathing in the crisp morning air and admiring the colourful trees, working out how all this beauty could be converted into poetry, dreaming about falling in love or being hopeful about the future. What is at work here is what Jung called 'active imagination' – 'a sequence of fantasies produced by deliberate concentration' (CW 9/I: para. 101). Active imagination is a technique that helps link the unconscious and consciousness; which gives it an outlet and a voice. Even though the process itself is 'deliberate', it nevertheless relies on the contents that stay below the surface of consciousness. The fantasies are framed and directed to an extent, but their origin – and the origin of creativity – is the unconscious.

At the crossing, your mood changed – and not consciously. Suddenly, you were surrounded by people. Inadvertently, you started copying their actions. When several of them crossed the road at the red light, you very nearly did the same, but stopped yourself at the last moment. In his writings, Jung repeatedly refers to crowd psychology; and particularly to the way our individuality is affected by the presence of other people. How do people interact with each other? How is their behaviour influenced by the vibes of communication and the necessity to fit in? The impulse to be the same as everyone else rather than different has a damaging effect on individual identity:

> Human beings have one faculty which, though it is of the greatest utility for collective purposes, is most pernicious for individuation, and that is the faculty of imitation. Collective psychology cannot dispense with imitation, for without it all mass organizations, the State and the social

order, are impossible. Society is organized indeed, less by law than by the propensity to imitation, implying equally suggestibility, suggestion, and mental contagion.

(CW 7: para. 242)

Moreover, every man is 'unconsciously a worse man when he is in society than when acting alone; for he is carried by society and to that extent relieved of his individual responsibility' (CW 7: para. 240). The presence of other people may be enough to encourage the state of *participation mystique* (the term, in fact, belongs to Lucien Levy-Bruhl) – a form of collective identification, an unconscious and automatic process. The mass 'is swayed by *participation mystique*, which is nothing other than an unconscious identity' (CW 9/I: para. 226). Your reaction to the people moving suddenly was to copy their actions in order to be like the rest of the group. Deep down, you are not as individual and unique as you may think. Your individuality is superseded and overwritten by social codes, and by the instinct of conformity.

The persona

When you entered the office building, you immediately became aware of the hierarchical structures and of your place in them. In other words, from an individual with his or her own plans and desires, you became a part of the system. This awareness of the system immediately activated what Jung called 'the persona' – the social mask that aids the individual in joining social structures and determining and accepting social roles (CW 7: para. 246). The persona is how we present ourselves to other people; it contains the qualities we want other people to see. More often than not, these qualities are related to popularity and success. The persona is one's public face, and we tend to worry about it – How do other people see us? Do they like us? Are we seen as friendly, interesting, or otherwise worthy of attention? In fact, attention plays a key role in these situations, and directly feeds into our self-esteem and confidence.

In social situations, we constantly have to make politically charged decisions in order to ensure our place in the hierarchy, as our survival and social progression depend on our conduct as well as the attractiveness of our public mask. We look around to see if there's anyone we should greet. When a colleague fails to say hello, we may start overthinking the situation, and getting worried about our social status. Is our status still intact? Do our colleagues (and particularly our bosses) like us? Why are several of them having lunch together and they did not invite me – is this a message? Are they trying to avoid me? Often, emotions that boil under the social mask are difficult to control as they revolve around the basic issues of survival, acceptance, rejection, public recognition and being an integral part of a social group. Often ego-consciousness struggles to deal with them because of the explosive combination of personal and archetypal elements in these emotions.

Jungians and post-Jungians have always emphasized the artificial nature of boundaries between people. The collective unconscious means that there is a common psychological ground that unites human beings. Despite the ego, which defines our individuality, and the personal unconscious, which contains our unique psychological issues, deep down we are still connected with other people. It is not easy to shake off this connection. Our internal world, Andrew Samuels argues, is also the interpersonal world; our thoughts and fantasies are dependent on our communication with others (Samuels, 2015: 129). Whatever we do, other people are always present in this.

In other words, the conscious 'I' is not fully in control of our reactions, neither when we daydreaming on our own, nor when we are surrounded by others and find ourselves submerging into the seductive world of *participation mystique*. It is important to note, however, that the ego is still important as it – to the best of its limited abilities, of course – attempts to separate consciousness from the unconscious, and to determine the shape of one's personality. As Mario Jacoby remarks, 'ego development implies, amongst other things, that one gets to know and learns to accept the genuine boundaries of one's person' (Jacoby, 2010: 88). By disentangling ourselves from the forces at work, we assert our individuality and uniqueness.

It is, however, often difficult to map the boundaries of one's consciousness. The persona – the attractive public mask – is one of the causes of this confusion. Jung attributes its existence of the persona to the collective rather than the personal psyche. Human beings like to present themselves to their surroundings in a certain way. The way we behave in public often differs from the way we are with our family, with whom we don't have to pretend to be nice and polite. Often people who are perceived as tyrants at work appear, behind closed doors, to be ideal mothers, fathers, husbands and wives.

The persona has an indispensable socio-psychological function – that of adaptation to external circumstances. As Frieda Fordham remarks, the persona is a necessity because it makes our communication with other human beings smoother as it cloaks the raw feelings and reactions into polite phrases and socially acceptable responses. People who reject the idea of a persona (perhaps because it feels like a false construct to them) tend to be 'gauche, to offend others, and to have difficulty establishing themselves in the world' (Fordham, 1966: 49). For instance, instead of punching someone when we feel like it because he or she jumped the queue, or bumping into people because they don't give way to us on a busy street, we tend to politely extract ourselves from potential conflict. Meanwhile, society views people who engage in open (and particularly physical) conflicts as those unable to develop and display a persona, and therefore keep such individuals from advancing on the social ladder.

Persona can take the form of a personal image, a career, a profession or an official role. For instance, people may want to be seen as a model mother, a benevolent boss, a cultured person, a successful scientist, an elegant dresser or a high earner. Despite its obvious usefulness and importance for adaptation, there are dangers associated with it; mainly because the desire for acceptance by the outer world often gets out of control, and turns into an obsession. The desire for success and status can be so powerful that the mask outgrows the individual and a set of artificial traits take over the ego. Jung writes:

> When we analyse the persona we strip off the mask, and discover that what seemed to be individual is at bottom collective; in other words, that the persona was only a mask of the collective psyche. Fundamentally the persona is nothing real: it is a compromise between individual and society as to what a man should appear to be. He takes a name, earns a title, exercises a function, he is this or that. In a certain sense all this is real, yet in relation to the essential individuality of the person concerned it is only a secondary reality, a compromise formation, in making which others often have a greater share than he. The persona is a semblance, a two-dimensional reality, to give it a nickname.
>
> (CW 7: para. 246)

The persona does not coincide with ego-consciousness. Instead, it is 'that which in reality one is not, but which oneself as well as others think one is' (CW 9/I: para. 221). In fact, the persona may start as representing ego-consciousness, but eventually inflation will distort it and fill it, for instance, with impossible grand visions of oneself, a fantasy version of one's status in the community and the world:

> Although the ego-consciousness is at first identical with the persona – that compromise role in which we parade before the community – yet the unconscious self can never be repressed to the point of extinction. Its influence is chiefly manifest in the special nature of the contrasting and compensating contents of the unconscious. The purely personal attitude of the conscious mind evokes reactions on the part of the unconscious, and these, together with personal repressions, contain the seeds of individual development in the guise of collective fantasies.
>
> (CW 7: para. 247)

In his writings, Jung repeatedly emphasizes the artificial nature of the persona and the fact that this artificiality comes from a social necessity. Society is a system of relationships and roles, and it needs to assign all individuals a purpose and a place. How valuable we are to other members of the system – in other words, our social status – depends on our ability to wear the mask well, and to ensure consistently high quality of performance in the roles we have been nominated to perform:

> Society expects, and indeed must expect, every individual to play the part assigned to him as perfectly as possible, so that a man who is a parson must not only carry out his official functions objectively, but must at all times and in all circumstances play the role of parson in a flawless manner. Society demands this as a kind of surety, each man must stand at his post, here a cobbler, there a poet. No man is expected to be both.
> (CW 7: para. 305)

No man is expected to be both a cobbler and a poet because the number of roles must be limited – society does not encourage an attitude to life that is too creative or too obscure. Everyone should clearly know who they are in the system in order for social processes to run smoothly. Meanwhile, society is far less interested in the issue of individual identity in the privacy of the individual's home because it does not work for the common good: 'To present an unequivocal face to the world is a manner of practical importance: the average man – the only kind society knows anything about – must keep his nose in one thing in order to achieve anything worthwhile, two would be too much. Our society is undoubtedly set on one such ideal' (CW 7: para. 305).

Our dependency on the superficial self-definition represented by our mask can be very powerful, and things go awry when the fantasy social image does not correspond with our actual achievements, or to the way we feel about ourselves. What if I am not a successful leader, popular friend, beautiful woman, intelligent conversationalist? Identification with a social role inevitably causes neuroses, Jung writes, because 'a man cannot get rid of himself in favour of an artificial personality without punishment' (CW 7: para. 307). This means that a strong man transforms into a mere child at home and 'his discipline in public goes miserably to pieces in private' (CW 7: para. 307).

Often, we are scared that one day we will be 'found out'; that someone will strip us down to our bare ego; that the public will uncover the small and vulnerable 'real me' who is not as attractive and influential as the mighty façade we present to society every day when we leave the house. The mask has to be 'perfect', and it is frightening to think that one day society will discover our lack of perfection, our personal flaws – the fact that we are just small people, mere mortals. Referring to this fear, Jolande Jacobi notes that the persona often serves as a protective shield which hides the inner self from 'prying eyes' (Jacobi, 1964: 350).

Mario Jacoby remarks that:

> identification with roles defined by society may not only procure the pseudo-satisfaction of a person's need for self-esteem – at the cost of his genuine individuality. There is also the danger that contents of an archetypal nature originating in the collective unconscious may lead to an inflation. [. . .] Since the ego, as the centre of consciousness, also exerts a reality-testing function, the inflation – that is, the blowing up of the ego with archetypal contents – leads to a loss of the sense of reality.
>
> (Jacoby, 2010: 88)

Jacoby rightly links this inflation by archetypal contents accompanied by the loss of reality to narcissistic fluctuations of self-esteem because 'a feeling of high personal value may result, for example, from an identification with the prestige inherent in a collective role: then I am someone, i.e., I am the president, the parson, the doctor' (2010: 87). The role becomes an exoskeleton as it replaces genuine self-esteem, which can only originate in feeling good about oneself while having respect for others.

The conflict between the inner world and the outer reality cloaked by persona is a staple subject of various popular narratives: novels, films and television series. In fact, the out-of-control persona makes for a good story which usually involves characters who dream of grandeur and fame. Many of the great classics, from Shakespeare's *Hamlet* (1603) to Dostoevsky's *The Idiot* (1869), explore a different conflict associated with the persona: they involve a protagonist who fights for authenticity, and for the right to feel and behave in a particular way. This 'other' way deviates from the rules and expectations of society – from the official (and, as these protagonists see it, corrupt and artificial) mask imposed on the individual by a culture, ideology or a political situation.

Literature has also been concerned with the development of the persona as a social adaptation mechanism, and particularly with its growth at the expense of empathy and compassion. Charles Dickens looks into this issue in many of his novels, including *Hard Times* (1864) and *Great Expectations* (1861). Invariably, for Dickens, the outer mask the individual is wearing is associated with class, wealth and social background.

Great Expectations

The tension between 'being yourself' and being part of the social hierarchy, with its habits, manners, language and rituals, is explored particularly well

Bystreetsky: *The mask*

in *Great Expectations*. The novel's protagonist is Pip – an orphan living with his bad-tempered sister and her kind blacksmith husband Joe in a village in Kent. The 'expectations' in the title hint at Pip's social ambition, and to his attempt to conquer London. The word also refers to the genre of the book – *Bildungsroman* – a novel focusing on a young person's education and maturation. At the start of the book, Pip has no ambition because his reality consists of the marsh village, his relatives and an assorted company of fairly eccentric guests who visit his sister's house. The boy's expectations from life are low. In fact, so naive and humble is he that he helps an escaped convict upon whom he stumbles on the marshes.

One day, however, he is invited for a play date with Estella, a beautiful girl adopted by a wealthy spinster, Miss Havisham. A resentful and frustrated jilted bride, Miss Havisham harbours a profound hatred for the male sex. She also intends to practise this hatred on the unsuspecting young man caught in her web. Little does Pip know that he is to become a plaything for Estella on whom to try out her manipulation techniques. After the first visit, Pip is overwhelmed by the brilliant world he has just seen and he is ashamed of his social class. In fact, he becomes aware of his social class only because Estella points it out to him by calling him a 'common labouring-boy':

> So, leaving word with the shopman on what day I was wanted at Miss Havisham's again, I set off on the four-mile walk to our forge; pondering, as I went along, on all I had seen, and deeply revolving that I was a common labouring-boy; that my hands were coarse; that my boots were thick; that I had fallen into a despicable habit of calling knaves Jacks; that I was much more ignorant than I had considered myself last night, and generally that I was in a low-lived bad way.
>
> (Dickens, 2003: 73)

This moment is the beginning of Pip's hope of acquiring a different persona. The one with which he grew up – that of a peasant, a common man – is no longer good enough after he has seen the way the upper classes live. He is disgusted with himself, and is ashamed of his speech and manners. The boy now believes that his happiness depends on attaining the persona of a gentleman, and detaching himself from his humble roots. He hopes that Miss Havisham has special plans for him – that she means to gentrify him, possibly to prepare him for the role of Estella's husband. Estella thus becomes a big part of Pip's imaginary future persona – that of a well-dressed nobleman with a beautiful woman on his arm to complement his splendour. In fact, his love for Estella may as well be his obsession with the image of a perfect gentleman.

However, Miss Havisham's plans do not involve Pip at all. Having shown him the glimpse of a resplendent lifestyle, she then tells the boy to go away and become Joe's apprentice. This is a serious blow for Pip, as it shatters the upper-class persona he was hoping to attain. His world is now reduced to his surroundings which are 'coarse and common'. He is ashamed of his home, and feels miserable about it. Pip is torn between his original humility (the inner world) and the possibility of becoming something bigger, someone more important (the outer mask):

> It is a most miserable thing to feel ashamed of home. There may be black ingratitude in the thing, and the punishment may be retributive and well deserved; but, that it is a miserable thing, I can testify.
>
> Home had never been a very pleasant place to me, because of my sister's temper. But, Joe had sanctified it, and I had believed in it. I had believed in the best parlour as a most elegant saloon; I had believed in the front door, as a mysterious portal of the Temple of State whose solemn opening was attended with a sacrifice of roast fowls; I had believed in the kitchen as a chaste though not magnificent apartment; I had believed in the forge as the glowing road to manhood and inde-pendence. Within a single year, all this was changed. Now, it was all coarse and common, and I would not have had Miss Havisham and Estella see it on any account.
>
> How much of my ungracious condition of mind may have been my own fault, how much Miss Havisham's, how much my sister's, is now of no moment to me or to any one. The change was made in me; the thing was done. Well or ill done, excusably or inexcusably, it was done.
>
> (Dickens, 2003: 122)

Pip spends some time being Joe's apprentice, but then something marvel-lous happens. A clerk arrives at the village to tell Pip that he has come into possession of a substantial fortune. The benefactor is not disclosed, and Pip automatically assumes that it is Miss Havisham, and that it is still part of her plan to create a perfect husband for Estella.

Pip is taken to London, where he finds new friends, rents a flat and orders many expensive clothes, jewellery and furnishings. He does not think of finding a job as the newly found wealth seems to be endless, and he fully assumes his idle 'nobleman' lifestyle. This persona keeps improving and becoming more or less how Pip initially imagined it to be – polished and agreeable. His new friend Herbert teaches the 'coarse labouring-boy' good table manners by pointing out to him that a gentleman should not put a din-ner knife in the mouth while eating; nor should he empty his glass 'as to turn it bottom upwards, with the rim on [his] nose' (Dickens, 2003: 206–7). Meanwhile, 'a dinner napkin will not go into a tumbler' (2003: 207).

Expensive furnishing, lavish dinners with oysters and newly acquired good manners soon confirmed Pip's fantasy of being a nobleman. Yet, Dickens astutely keeps noting how uneasy Pip feels at the thought of losing this mask; how he suspects that one day he will be discovered. After all, his shiny new outer image is not something with which he was born, but something he has recently acquired. So afraid is Pip of the possibility of being found out that any reminder of his peasant roots terrifies him. When he receives the news that Joe is coming to London and wants to visit him, Pip plunges into despair. So little does he want to see Joe that he is prepared to pay him money to keep him away:

> I received this letter by post on Monday morning, and therefore its appointment was for next day. Let me confess exactly, with what feelings I looked forward to Joe's coming.
>
> Not with pleasure, though I was bound to him by so many ties; no; with considerable disturbance, some mortification, and a keen sense of incongruity. If I could have kept him away by paying money, I certainly would have paid money. My greatest reassurance was, that he was coming to Barnard's Inn, not to Hammersmith, and consequently would not fall in Bentley Drummle's way. I had little objection to his being seen by Herbert or his father, for both of whom I had a respect; but I had the sharpest sensitiveness as to his being seen by Drummle, whom I held in contempt. So, throughout life, our worst weaknesses and meannesses are usually committed for the sake of the people whom we most despise.
>
> (Dickens, 2003: 252)

Eventually, the secret of Pip's mystery wealth is revealed: the money came from Abel Magwitch, the convict helped by Pip on the marshes. Magwitch was captured and sent to New South Wales, where he worked hard to make money in order to transform Pip into a gentleman. He then comes to England only to see Pip, knowing that he would be executed if captured. All these revelations shock the young man, whose inflated vision of himself is now fractured. The mask is revealed to have nothing to do with Miss Havisham. Not only is it tainted with the associations with a criminal, but it also has origins in the boy's original character traits – empathy, openness and kindness.

Magwitch is eventually caught, which means that his fortune will now go to the crown. The loss of the precious self-image has a profound effect on the young man: after Magwitch is executed and Herbert takes up a position in Cairo, Pip falls seriously ill. He is also facing prison for his debts. However, he is saved by Joe, who nurses him back to health and pays off his debts.

When the worst part of the illness is over and Pip wakes up from the delirium, he apologizes to Joe for not maintaining a good relationship with his family. It can be said that Pip's illness is a transitional – liminal – state in which his psyche is trying to grow a new, more authentic and realistic self-image – instead of the inflated old one that had been damaged and then destroyed.

Pip's latest persona may not be terribly exciting or lavish, but it is much healthier because it is not based on a fantasy but on a pragmatic approach to life: he becomes a clerk to Clarriker and Co., a merchant business. His progress is slow but steady: after many years of learning the trade and working a clerk, he becomes a partner in the House. Having learned from his previous mistakes, Pip is now realistic about his career and social position: both are now earned, not bestowed upon him. He also gradually deals with his debts and pays off his creditors. Dickens's moral lesson here is that this kind of persona is more genuine and therefore closer to how individuals feel about themselves. It does not have to be faked or inflated because it is real; it is based on actual (although perhaps not very glorious) personal achievements:

> I must not leave it to be supposed that we were ever a great House, or that we made mints of money. We were not in a grand way of business, but we had a good name, and worked for our profits, and did very well. We owed so much to Herbert's ever cheerful industry and readiness, that I often wondered how I had conceived that old idea of his inaptitude, until I was one day enlightened by the reflection, that perhaps the inaptitude had never been in him at all, but had been in me.
>
> (Dickens, 2003: 555)

The finale of *Great Expectations* emphasizes the importance of self-reflection coupled with a realistic approach to life. The deflation of the mask of an idle nobleman and its replacement with the image of a hard-working man (the bourgeois ideal, of course!) is the very aim of the lengthy and torturous lesson meted out to Pip. Jung's advice in relation to persona is similar to that of Dickens in *Great Expectations*: for the purpose of individuation and self-realization, it is important for the individual 'to distinguish between what he is and what he appears to himself and others' (CW 7: para. 195). The same story can, of course, be analysed from a Freudian perspective: as a harsh way of adapting to reality through renunciation of fantasy and reduction of narcissism. In any case, whether we examine Pip's developmental trajectory through the lens of individuation and persona (Jung) or adaptation to reality and narcissism (Freud), the goal of his journey is become more aware of the outside world, and to develop a more believable social mask which is closer to the individual's inner reality.

The self

Whereas the ego is the centre of consciousness and contains our unique personality traits, the self is the unattainable personality centre uniting the different parts of the psyche. Jung writes: 'The ego is, by definition, subordinate to the self and is related to it like a part to the whole. Inside the field of consciousness it has, as we say, free will. [. . .] it finds its limits outside the field of consciousness in the subjective inner world, where it comes into conflict with the facts of the self' (CW 9/II: para. 5).

The self is connected with the collective while the ego distinguishes the individual from collectivity, both internal and external. It was also defined by Jung as one of the archetypes as this complex and vague idea of wholeness and unity often appears in dreams, narratives and artwork in a range of forms, including ritual symbols with complex patterns such as mandalas, or spiritual teachers such as Buddha or Jesus.

Like any other psychic organ, it has a function, and this function is closely related to the individuation process. It fact, a glimpse of the self which you may catch when you move nearer to the psychic equilibrium is the very goal of the individuation process, which is a process of becoming yourself while also being part of your society (discussed in detail in Chapter 3). Jung keeps noting that, unfortunately, 'our Western mind' is so orientated towards the outer world, with its pressures, successes, bustle and hustle (and the persona, one may surmise), that it becomes separated from the self by a wall built by consciousness trying to keep away all irrational contents.

So preoccupied are we with the rational way of doing things that we don't even have a name for 'the union of opposites through the middle path, that most fundamental item of inward experience . . .' (CW 7: para. 327). The Western individual somehow thinks that the ego *is* the whole personality, and makes the serious mistake of splitting himself from the collective man a part of whom he is (CW 8: para. 557). However, even when we are not aware of the universal human being in us called the self, or when we reject it, we are still being led and advised by it, because its goal is 'the ultimate integration of conscious and unconscious, or better, the assimilation of the ego to a wider personality' (CW 8: para. 306).

Of course, psychic wholeness can never be attained because, Jung argues, consciousness is too small to comprehend the vastness of the psyche (CW 14: para. 759). One could say that the self is a process rather than a goal. However, being aware of the existence and importance of this psychic organ would allow modern individuals to attain a degree of inner peace as well as better relationships with others. The fast-paced modern way of living, which demands time-saving and efficiency, does not have a place or time for contemplating the self, and we end up looking outwards rather than inwards. There are various ways of aiming towards, and partially achieving, psychic wholeness, including mindfulness, meditation and yoga (all of which often use symbols to help you perceive and accept the self). However, Jung keeps warning us, the important thing is to be aware of the trappings of the ego, which is too sure of its uniqueness and supremacy, for there are other, larger powers within the human psyche, and neglecting these can lead to very unpleasant discoveries about both the outside world and one's own character.

Summary

According to Jung, human personality is multi-layered. Although we tend to perceive the centre of consciousness – the ego – as in charge of our reactions and performance of daily routines, other significant phenomena, notably the persona and the self, are often also involved. The persona ensures our adaptation to the norms and requirements of society, while the self connects consciousness with the unconscious and links together the different parts of the psyche, thus creating an underlying base for its unity.

5   Jung on creativity

Jungian Analytical Psychology has proved to be particularly popular in the arts and humanities. Its core concepts – and particularly archetypes and individuation – have been used by authors, screenwriters, artists and critics to construct stories and symbols as well as to reflect on the creative process.

This chapter shows the numerous ways in which archetypes and other Jungian ideas can be used to create and examine works of art and social processes. It starts with an overview of the differences between Jungian and Freudian schools in their treatment of creativity and its products, then moves on to discuss Jungian approaches to literary and film criticism, and, finally, explores the new areas of Jungian film studies and 'archetypal marketing'.

Creativity and the artist

Art criticism and narrative analysis have been dominated by Freudian and post-Freudian ideas since the beginning of the twentieth century. In particular, literary studies and film criticism (including its feminist branch) have been reliant on Lacanian concepts, including the 'three orders' (the Imaginary, the Symbolic, and the Real), the mirror stage, *jouissance* and *objet a*.

By contrast, artists and writers have been traditionally more interested than critics in Jungian ideas. This is probably because Jung offers a more optimistic and respectful view of creativity and its products than Freud, who sees it as mainly a by-product of neurosis.

Signs and symbols

One of the fundamental differences between Jungian and Freudian theories is their treatment of symbols. Freud preferred to interpret them literally, and attached a single interpretation, whereas Jung's approach consisted of offering a range of possible interpretations – meanings on a variety of levels. He called this process *amplification* (discussed in detail in Chapter 1).

Freudian psychology traditionally concentrates on retrospective elements of the work of art: the artist's childhood and biography, sexuality, relationships with parents and the opposite sex, etc. Most of the Freudian studies of works of art in some way or another concern the artist's strong and unfulfilled desires – pleasure and sexuality, envy and greed, aggression and guilt. In other words, creativity is a way of sublimating (transforming) unpleasant and dangerous human instincts into socially acceptable forms: a painting, a song, a poem or a novel.

Freud saw the relationship between the form of the phenomenon (the signifier) and its content (the signified), as fixed, at least within his own interpretive framework, as if it were closed and resembled in its simplicity and precision the traffic light system (which has one possible set of interpretations). Long after his dramatic break-up with Freud, Jung kept commenting on how unsuitable Freud's reductive methods were for analysing works of art and literature. He complained that Freud mistook symbols for signs, arguing that the imagery and narratives the unconscious comes up with, when it shows us dreams and helps us write novels, are too complex and multifaceted to be given a singular interpretation:

> The true symbol differs essentially from this, and should be understood as an expression of an intuitive idea that cannot yet be formulated in any other or better way. When Plato, for instance, puts the whole problem of the theory of knowledge in his parable of the cave, or when Christ expresses the idea of the Kingdom of Heaven in parables, these are genuine and true symbols, that is, attempts to express something for which no verbal concept yet exists. If we were to interpret Plato's metaphor in Freudian terms we would naturally arrive at the uterus, and would have proved that even a mind like Plato's was still struck on a primitive level of infantile sexuality.
>
> (CW 15: para. 105)

For instance, in his essay about the works of the Russian author Fyodor Dostoevsky (1821–1881), 'Dostoevsky and Parricide' (1928), Freud goes so far as to argue that the writer's epilepsy was linked to his desire to kill his father – the desire at the heart of the Oedipus complex (SE, XXI: 181–4). Freud also traces the motif of parricide in Dostoevsky's novel *The Brothers Karamazov* (1880) to the writer's (unproven) desire to murder his father (SE, XXI: 185). According to Freud, the Russian author channelled all his angry thoughts about his father into his characters, thus flushing the negative emotions out of his system and publicly admitting his Oedipal guilt. He also suppressed his 'masculine' aggression and became 'feminine' and 'masochistic' in his attempt to deny the existence of his own anger, jealousy and desire (SE, XXI: 185). Thus, in Freud's view, Dostoevsky's epileptic fits are caused by guilt and can be seen as a form of self-punishment and even as suicidal attempts.

Equally problematic and far-fetched is Freud's analysis of Leonardo da Vinci's creative life. In 'Leonardo Da Vinci and a Memory of His Childhood' (1910), Freud links the painter's talent to his repressed homosexuality as well as to early Oedipal desires. To support his conclusions, Freud cites a dream Leonardo recalls having as a child, in which a large vulture came to the artist as he laid in his cradle, and inserted its tail into his mouth. Predictably, Freud interprets the tail as a penis and implies that the young artist dreamt of a sexual act (SE, XI: 78). Freud's tone shows that he has no doubts that Leonardo had sexual desire for his mother which, when repressed, turned first into homosexuality and eventually sought a creative outlet.

By contrast, Jung and his disciples emphasize the importance of respect for the unconscious and its symbols. Human beings, Erich Neumann argues, create symbols because they help us make meaning out of the messy, unpredictable, impulsive dark whirlwind of unconscious forces: 'The psychic undercurrents which determine man's feeling and image of the world are manifested through colours and forms, tones and words, which crystallize into symbolic spiritual figures expressing man's relation both to the archetypal world and to the world in which he lives' (Neumann, 1959: 84). Moreover, man is the co-creator of his narratives: he helps the unconscious shape them:

> In the original situation man's emotion in the presence of the numinosum leads to expression, for the unconscious, as part of its creative function, carries with it its own expression. But the emotional drives which move the group and the individual within it must not be conceived a dynamic without content. For every symbol, like every archetype, has a specific content, and when the whole of a man is seized by the collective unconscious, this means his consciousness too. Consequently we find from the very start that the creative function of the psyche is accompanied by a reaction of consciousness, which seeks, at first in slight degree but then increasingly, to understand, to interpret, and to assimilate the thing by which it was at first overwhelmed. Thus at a very early stage there is a relative fixation of expression and style, and so definite traditions arise.
> (Neumann, 1959: 85)

Jungian film critics have been particularly concerned with the interpretive freedom of symbolism. In his article 'Jung/Sign/Symbol/Film' (1979), Don Fredericksen compares the Freudian and Jungian takes on signs and symbols. He agrees with Jung that Freud's analysis of works of art is essentially semiotic (and, as such, reductive), and regards Jung's treatment of creativity and its products as symbolic (i.e., allowing interpretive freedom). A sign has only one possible meaning, while a symbol can have a whole hierarchy of interpretations. Fredericksen demonstrates 'our need and our capacity to be open to meaning – filmic and otherwise – of a kind and in places where semiotic attitudes have not previously found it' (Hauke and Alister, 2001: 17). He also points out that, by attaching ourselves to particular critical opinions, 'we are denying ourselves a sense of meaning – and a wisdom – at once very old and very alive in the contemporary world, including the world of film' (2001: 17). Interpretive freedom is particularly important in film and television criticism, as moving-image narratives do not lend themselves easily to singular interpretations.

Creativity

Freudian analytical tradition sees creativity in a pessimistic light; as a vehicle for getting rid of unwanted thoughts and feelings. To use Jung's expression, for Freud 'every artist is a narcissist' (CW 15: para. 79). As such, art can be analysed and explained away. By contrast, for Jung, the artist expresses 'the unconscious desire of the times' (CW 15: para. 153). It is as if, as a creative person, you do not choose to make a work of art, but rather a work of art chooses you as its vehicle. This is due to the fact that, to a large extent, Jungian and post-Jungian theory is far more modern than its Freudian counterpart as it has more respect for 'the other': the unconscious, creativity, fantasy and deviations from society's vision of reality – from the norms of adaptation (Samuels, 2015: 214–15).

Freudian theory postulates that most collective phenomena are conscious and they shape and change the often subconscious personal phenomena – instincts, feelings, fears, etc. The collective is that civilizing, reality-defining body that brings individuals to their senses whenever order needs to be preserved or restored (which is pretty much all the time). The collective is thus seen as oppressive, structured and uncompromising. It represents the systemic element in society, whereas the artist is a person driven by the uniquely personal unconscious impulses.

Creativity, Freud argues in *Beyond the Pleasure Principle* (1920) is a grown-up version of child's play, a way of sublimating the discomfort associated with the infant's introduction to reality. For instance, it is difficult for a baby to accept separation – even temporary – from its mother, so it re-enacts the event in an attempt to better have control over it. Play becomes therapeutic. Freud writes: 'It is clear that in their play children repeat everything that has made an impression on them in real life, and that in doing so they abreact the strength of the impression and, as one might put it, make themselves master of the situation' (SE, XVIII: 17). Grown-ups simply turn this tension between the pleasure principle and reality into works of art. This means, Freud notes, that even such a contentious thing as the pleasure principle can serve a good purpose (SE, XVIII: 17). He even proposes a theory of aesthetics that would take into account the supremacy of the pleasure principle and would not refer to anything outside it.

This idea was later expanded by many talented psychotherapists, including the English paediatrician Donald Winnicott, who coined the term 'transitional object' as a key part of his account of the origins of creativity in humans; and the American psychiatrist George Vaillant, who believed that sublimation – that is, creative transformation of personal problems into works of art – was the highest defence mechanism.

One of Freud's followers, the child psychoanalyst Melanie Klein (1882–1960), also regarded creativity as a sublimation of 'dark instincts' – in her case, these were primarily anger and guilt. People become creative out of the necessity to get rid of the sadness that accompanies the demands and pressures of living in 'reality' and repress the drive to the pleasure principle. In her essay 'Infantile Anxiety-Situations Reflected in a Work of Art and in the Creative Impulse' (1929), Klein recalls that one of her patients, a painter Ruth Kjär (Ruth Weber-Kiaer), had spent many years being seriously depressed. She also loved art. One day, her brother-in-law had to sell a painting which had previously been lent to her and occupied a prominent place in her living room. Looking at the blank space on the wall, where the picture had previously hung, made her particularly sad, until her husband found a solution – he suggested that she painted something herself. The result was a beautiful picture of a woman. Everyone – including the completely untrained artist – was shocked at this suddenly revealed talent (Klein, 1975c: 216). Eventually, Ruth paints her mother, who for all these years had been the real cause of her sadness, anger and guilt:

> This lady has a long time before she must put her lips to the cup of renunciation. Slim, imperious, challenging, she stands there with a moonlight-coloured shawl draped over her shoulders: she has the effect of a magnificent woman of primitive times, who could any day engage in combat with the children of the desert with her naked hands. What a chin! What a force there is in the haughty gaze!
> 'The blank space has been filled.'
>
> (Klein, 1975c: 217)

Jungian psychology rescues creativity from this dynamic, and takes some of the focus away from the individual's sexuality, sibling envy, early traumas and impressions, and any other retrospective issues, and directs it towards the collective aspects of the individual's existence. This is because it sees the unconscious as consisting of two levels: the personal and the collective. Thus, on the 'invisible' level, people are influenced by the collective unconscious; and they are also shaped by their immediate environment and the wider society. As such, collective influences go far beyond the punitive role of the superego or patriarchal structures. Far from theorizing the unconscious as a dumping box for socially undesirable traits such as personal guilt, and as something that can be managed and controlled, it becomes a vast space, a sort of psychic internet, in which traits common for all human beings are shared.

According to Jung, works of art are born in response to social challenges and political necessities. Although not entirely impersonal, they nevertheless reflect the spirit of their times more so than do their authors' Oedipal problems. He argues in his essay 'Psychology and Literature':

> Great poetry draws its strengths from the life of mankind, and we completely miss its meaning if we try to derive it from personal factors. Whenever the collective unconscious becomes a living experience and is brought to bear upon the conscious outlook of an age, this event is a creative act which is of importance for the whole epoch. A work of art is produced which may truthfully be called a message to generations of men.
>
> (CW 15: para. 153)

Although Jung admits that there are novels, poems and songs that are consciously planned; in many cases, the artist has little control over the creative process. The work of art, Jung argues, grows out of its creator rather like a tree that draws its nourishment from the artist's psyche. It is a force 'that achieves its end either with tyrannical might or with the subtle cunning of the nature herself, quite regardless of the personal fate of the man who is its vehicle' (CW 15: para. 114). The work of art is a 'living thing implanted in human psyche' (CW 15: para. 114), and the tree grows out of 'the nourishing soil' of the collective unconscious (CW 15: para. 121). This is a powerful metaphor to describe the creative process because it renders the sheer force with which creativity escapes the mind of the artist, causing him or her to lose control over the process.

Like this, the work of art is born out of its creator against his will, and in response to the current social climate. It may resonate in the author's personal unconscious, of course – or even come out of his personal problems. Yet, when he feels the need to create, the artist only answers the call of the collective unconscious; his issues only naturally grow out from the deepest problems of his society. Through the artist, the unconscious speaks and the collective expresses itself. The work of art becomes an autonomous complex – an independent constellation of information in the psyche; a sort of galaxy floating in the unconscious (CW 15: para. 122). One can recognize it and make it conscious; in fact, the very act of creating a work of art takes the complex out of the depths of the unconscious, and illuminates it by transforming it into something useful.

Imbued with this social significance, works of art originate in the collective psyche, and in response to the social and political problems of the times. It is as if the collective unconscious has an educational purpose and it realizes its purpose via its chosen vehicle – the artist. Disturbed by historical events, primordial images seek expression, and the artist gives them shape by translating them into the language of the present (CW 15: para. 130). The artist's task is thus to recognize and seize the image, and to transform it into a message which could be understood by his contemporaries (CW 15: para. 130). This is a two-way process, as creativity also gives the creator a sense of accomplishment and power:

> Whoever speaks in primordial images speaks with a thousand voices; he enthrals and overpowers, while at the same time he lifts the idea he is seeking to express out of the occasional and the transitory into the realm of the over-enduring. He transmutes our personal destiny into the destiny of mankind, and evokes in us all those beneficent forces that ever and anon have enabled humanity to find a refuge from every peril and to outlive the longest night.
>
> (CW 15: para. 129)

All this may sound good, but the might of the collective coupled with unstoppable creativity, however, affects the artist's life and mental health. Both make the creative person vulnerable and psychologically unstable, which explains why so many artists fail to have what is seen as 'a normal life' by the majority of people. 'The divine frenzy of the artist' – Jung writes – 'comes perilously close to a pathological state, though the two things are not identical' (CW 15: para. 122). Creative people are thus mere vehicles for this unstoppable energy that demands to be let out. It is no wonder, then, that artists often forget reality altogether, and become wholly engaged in the process of harvesting the trickster impulse and rescuing it from the depths of the unconscious.

Thus, a creative person becomes a sort of martyr and prophet, seized by an invisible force that has chosen him or her as a spokesperson to reveal the truth about the world to the people. This is a more flattering vision of the artist and the arts than the view that creativity is the result of issues in the person's sexual development, or a suppressed desire to have sex with the mother.

The Jungian view of creativity also emphasizes the social and collective significance of works of art instead of relegating them exclusively to the realm of the personal or turning them into mere waste bins for problematic psychological contents.

Jungian art and criticism: images and narratives

One of the key aspects of Analytical Psychology is its ability to organize and manage narratives. The individuation process itself is a loose narrative structure comprising various basic human experiences, including leaving (and dealing with) one's parents, falling in love and growing old. Building a novel or a screenplay around the individuation milestones would make it relatable to the general public, for its structure would reflect the experiences shared by everyone. Unlike the Oedipus complex, which is the core narrative of Freudian theory, the individuation process is a flexible tool and comprises a variety of possible paths. Moreover, the Jungian journey of self-discovery is prospective rather than retrospective, as it is more interested in the possibilities that lie ahead than in the defence mechanisms that formed in the past, and are now played out in our relationships with others. As such, Jung's ideas influenced a number of prominent creatives, including the artist Jackson Pollock (who was inspired by the Jungian analysis he underwent in the 1940s) and the novelist John Fowles.

Painting with Jung

Analytical Psychology attaches special significance to the image, and several of Jung's disciples wrote about twentieth-century art. The anti-realistic, anti-rational art movements of modernity that reflected the fragmented, complex twentieth-century world both fascinated and alarmed Jung's disciples Aniela Jaffé, Erich Neumann, Joseph Henderson and Jung himself. The interest was mutual: several abstract expressionist painters, including Jackson Pollock, Mark Rothko and Adolph Gottlieb, were influenced by Jung's theories, and applied them to their art.

Jungians were particularly interested in the irrational, messy nature of modern literary and art movements. Modernity, with its complex urban environments and destructive technology, inspired both fascination and fear. Throughout the last quarter of the nineteenth and the entire twentieth century, art and literature had been reflecting this dichotomy, producing symbols and narratives that showed the confusion and psychological fragmentation experienced by the individual in the fast-paced, ever-changing, hostile world.

Bystreetsky: *Creativity and the artist*

Echoing Jung's views on the dark and formidable might of creativity, Erich Neumann writes in *Art and the Creative Unconscious* that the artists of modernity are swayed by powers they are unable to understand or control. Moreover, since the collective unconscious has an external aspect, that is, it is linked to our collective behaviour, and to our mass reactions, historical events and political change are bound to find their expression in works of art. For instance, when the world is perceived by individuals as hostile and 'broken', when people feel increasingly isolated from each other and the sense of community is lost, the unconscious comes up with fragmented, erratic images, disconnected narratives and dissonant sounds (which have been consistently present in modernist art, literature and music). Neumann tells us that this chaos filters through the artists, often affecting their mental health, and perception and acceptance of reality:

> The modern painters of the last sixty years have been captured by a power which threatens to destroy them. These painters are not masters in the old sense, but victims, even when they dominate the situation. Because the form of the outside world has been shattered, an identifiable and learnable artistic technique has almost ceased to exist. All these artists suffer the demonic violence of the inward powers. Whether they are driven like Munch by solitute and sickness, like Van Gogh into the release of madness, like Gauguin to the distant isles of primitivism, or like Picasso into the amorphous world of inner transformation – their despair and the strain under which they work contrast sharply with the tranquility of earlier artists, who felt that they were carrying on a tradition.
>
> (Neumann, 1959: 117)

Neumann paints a picture of almost Christ-like figures who have to suffer for their art: 'We find in Kubin and the early Klee the grotesque distortion, the anxiety and distress, that come of inundation by the unconscious' (1959: 117–18).

Aniela Jaffé also links the bizarre forms and disordered technique of modern painting to the artists' immersion into the collective unconscious. She notes that Pollock's pictures are 'charged with boundless emotional vehemence' as they look like a 'glowing lava stream of colours, lines, planes, and points' (Jung & von Franz, 1964: 308–9). In rejecting form, the artist goes back to the alchemical *prima materia*, the pre-civilized, pre-logical chaos; he paints 'the nothing that is everything' – that is, 'the unconscious itself' (1964: 309).

A similar sentiment was expressed by Jung with regard to Picasso's style. Having noted the abundance of symbolic content in Picasso's paintings,

Jung compared the way in which it was expressed in the artist's work to his patients' pictures. Both Picasso and Jung's patients did not depict any unified 'harmonious feeling-tone', but rather 'contradictory feelings or even a complete lack of feeling' (CW 15: para. 208). Such an art is 'schizophrenic' rather than 'neurotic' because the former abandons the idea of meaning altogether while the latter still attempts to create meaning out of chaos, and to communicate it to the audience (CW 15: para. 209). Modernity, Jung implies, has descended into the unconscious underworld, and its schizophrenic, unstructured imagery is the result of this.

Jung, Neumann and Jaffé do not pass judgement on the quality of the works produced by modern painters. Nor are they interested in their childhoods, as Freudians might have been. In fact, elsewhere Neumann promotes respect for the symbols coming out of the unconscious, and warns of the dangers of interpreting them in literal or sexual terms (his defence of Leonardo's vulture dream is discussed in Chapter 1). The critic's task, as Jungians see it, is to explore the work of art as a medium between the outside world and the collective unconscious, and not as a seat of the artist's personal issues. In the creative process, the artist is merely a channel chosen by the unconscious to express universal issues encased into specific concerns of the time. As such, he is a recorder of history and societal issues, and not merely an individual sublimating his or her Oedipal problems onto a canvas or paper.

Writing with Jung: literature and literary criticism

Analytical Psychology's inherent respect for the spiritual component of creative products also attracted the attention of writers and literary critics. A number of authors, including the novelist John Fowles and poet Seamus Heaney, have been using Jung to bring back myth and meaning into contemporary life. For instance, Heaney read a number of Jung's texts and mentioned his interest in Jung in a number of interviews (Dennison, 2015: 57). His poetry is full of archetypal symbolism, from the metaphorical representations of the unconscious to various portrayals of the self. Similarly, John Fowles used Jung's ideas both to structure his narratives and to explore the nature of truth and meaning in postmodern life, particularly in *The Magus* (1965) and *A Maggot* (1985).

Unlike Freudian art and literary critics, the Jungians have not been focusing on just one narrative (the Oedipus complex). They have been more interested in the structuring potential of Analytical Psychology, and particularly in the individuation process (as the skeleton for the story) and the archetypes (as the milestones, as well as metaphors for obstacles on the hero's path). Modernity, with its fragmented, fast-paced life and equally fragmented narratives, drew Jung's attention because it showed a lack of structure – as well as the hidden, dangerous yearning for a unifying structure – in times of political and social upheaval.

For instance, Jung is baffled by James Joyce's *Ulysses*. He calls the meandering, pessimistic narrative of *Ulysses* 'boring', compares it to a 'tapeworm', and notes the intentional absence of logic and order in it. Similar to his views on Picasso, Jung observes that the book itself is not the product of one schizophrenic mind, but rather of the whole schizophrenic culture (CW 15: para. 174). It is simply not possible to produce a well-woven picture of reality out of the world which has just been shattered by a war, and transformed forever by rapid technological change.

At the same time, Jung and his disciples emphasize the archetypal, eternal nature of narratives. Archetypes and individuation are popular concepts because they embody the human yearning for order and structure. This is why it is important to always look beyond the biography of the author, Jung warns. When the archetypal makeup of a story is reduced to a personal experience, 'the . . . vision loses its primordial quality and becomes nothing but a symptom: the teeming chaos shrinks to the proportions of a psychic disturbance' (CW 15: para. 146).

This 'structuralist' potential of Jungian ideas was utilized by literary theorists and mythology specialists such as Northrop Frye and Joseph Campbell. In his book *Anatomy of Criticism: Four Essays* (1957), Northrop Frye weaves archetypal criticism into his grand vision of themes, symbols and genres in literature, and Joseph Campbell famously uses Jung to create an all-encompassing list of themes and motifs in mythology and folklore. Both approaches have proved to be very popular, and have been employed to explore all kinds of narratives, but one needs to be careful not to turn them into reductive methods so that that the critic would be looking for superficial structures and formulaic meanings.

Jungian film studies

Psychoanalytic film theory has historically been grounded in Freud and Lacan as well as British object relations theories. However, by the early 1980s psychoanalytic cultural criticism was running out of steam, despite the fact that there remained cadres of scholars who continue to wave the psychoanalytic flag. Some early signs began to emerge that a renaissance in Freudian and Lacanian thinking was beginning. It was also in that period that Jungian film studies began to take shape.

Film criticism has proved to be one of the most popular and prolific branches of Analytical Psychology outside the clinic. Even though Jungian and post-Jungian concepts are still new to most academics and film critics, things are gradually changing, and Jungian film studies is a now a fast-growing academic field. It has taken two main directions: narrative analysis (John Izod, Terrie Waddell, Helena Bassil-Morozow) and phenomenological criticism (Luke Hockley, Greg Singh). One of the pioneers of the field, the filmmaker and theorist Christopher Hauke, explores both how films are made and their effects on audiences, in both narrative and phenomenological aspects.

The narrative group has traditionally been paying more attention to the structural, symbolic and semiotic heritage of Jungian thought, while the phenomenological cluster is more interested in the meaning-making and therapeutic properties of the cinematic experience. In fact, the two groups have been doing important work and exploring film from two complementary angles: the making of the structure and the birth of meaning. Both are firmly rooted in Jung's idea of the collective unconscious as both a source of emotional trouble and a well of therapeutic experience. They also share the central Jungian interest in the 'individuating golden mean' – the border between the personal and the collective in human experience. One of the central institutions of modern life, due to its mass characters and technological possibilities, the visual image offers limitless opportunities for examining and negotiating this border.

One of the first authors to explore the usefulness of Jungian theory for film studies was Don Fredericksen. In his article 'Jung/Sign/Symbol/Film' (1979), Fredericksen maps out the differences between Freudian and Jungian psychology regarding creativity and works of art. It is the battle between the semiotic and the symbolic attitudes – the first interprets narrative elements and metaphors as signs, and the second as symbols. The difference between the two lies in the amount of interpretive freedom, and in the number of interpretations possible, for each symbol. Following Jung, Fredericksen hopes to demonstrate 'our need and our capacity to be open to meaning – filmic and otherwise – of a kind and in places where semiotic attitudes have not previously found it' (Hauke and Alister, 2001: 17). Fredericksen insists that fashionable interpretations and notions of meaning, instead of expanding and enlightening the world, make it look narrow, and by this narrowness 'we are denying ourselves a sense of meaning – and a wisdom – at once very old and very alive in the contemporary world, including the world of film' (2001: 17).

Another pioneer of Jungian film studies is John Izod. His more recent publications include *Myth, Mind and the Screen: Understanding the Heroes of Our Time* (2001) and *Screen, Culture, Psyche: A Post-Jungian Approach to Working with the Audience* (2006). Izod draws his analyses of screen texts from the concepts of individuation, archetypal imagery and creative possibilities of the unconscious. For instance, in *Screen, Culture,*

Psyche (2006), he traces character transformation throughout Stanley Kubrick's *Eyes Wide Shut* (1999), Bernardo Bertolucci's *Stealing Beauty* (1996), *The Dreamers* (2003), *Besieged* (1998), and Andrew Niccol's *Simone* (2002). He also discusses the use of myths in British documentaries of the 1980s and 1990s, and the mythology and archetypalism of the Western world/culture.

Izod's writings can be grouped together with two other Jungian film authors: Terrie Waddell and Helena Bassil-Morozow. Terrie is a former actress, and now an academic author and lecturer. Her publications include a range of edited collections and monographs, the most notable being *Mis/takes: Archetype, Myth and Identity in Screen Fiction* (2006) and *Wild/lives: Trickster, Place and Liminality on Screen* (2009). In these books, Waddell explores a range of archetypes (and particularly their female incarnations) in contemporary film and television. For instance, in *Mis/takes* she discusses the ways in which contemporary mythology, as outlined in film, reflects the identity issues of the individual as well as the fundamental problems of contemporary society.

Helena Bassil-Morozow is another author who concentrates on the archetypal aspect of visual narratives. Her publications on film include the monographs *Tim Burton: The Monster and the Crowd* (2010), *The Trickster in Contemporary Film* (2012) and *The Trickster and the System: Identity and Agency in Contemporary Society* (2015). Like many post-Jungian authors, her research is based on the premise that mass media is a direct reflection of the collective psyche. More immediate and accessible than any other art form, it faithfully reflects the emotional and intellectual condition of the contemporary Western individual. Interestingly enough, both Waddell and Bassil-Morozow concentrate their works on the trickster figure, as it reflects the spirit of post-industrial time and shows the changes in the collective psyche more faithfully than any other image. The trickster represents pure change, pure movement, which makes 'him' a suitable metaphor for the description of the fast-paced environments and lifestyles of Western societies.

In the world of Jungian film criticism, Christopher Hauke's vision of cinema is probably the most all-encompassing as he is an academic author and lecturer, a filmmaker and a psychotherapist. The two collections he co-edited with his colleagues, Ian Alister and Luke Hockley respectively, *Jung and Film: Post-Jungian Takes on the Moving Image* (2001) and *Jung and Film II: The Return* (2011), brought together a range of Jungian film scholars in the hope of outlining the emerging academic discipline.

In his most recent book, *Visible Mind: Movies, Modernity and the Unconscious* (2014), Christopher Hauke discusses films in terms of their mythological value for the contemporary individual. He argues that cinematic narratives hold therapeutic value which is as generally symbolic as it is dependent on personal circumstances. Cinematic narratives, Hauke states, are contemporary versions of eternal myths. People have always used tales as meaning-making devices, and moving images are particularly good for this purpose. Cinema has the possibility 'of becoming an imaginal space' and film watching offers 'a special place where psyche can come alive, be experienced and be commented upon'. Moreover, as self-discovery is often a complex and painful process, 'popular cultural forms such as cinema can provide the holding necessary for intense experiences, making them more accessible and more bearable' (Hauke, 2014: 4).

Luke Hockley and Greg Singh can be said to comprise the 'phenomeno-logical' wing of Jungian film studies, which is more interested in the ways film images influence the audience than in the narrative construction aspect of films. They write about a number of issues concerning emotional exchange between the screen and the audience: construction of meaning, therapeutic effect of cinematic narratives, projective–introjective exchange, and identity and identification in relation to screen images.

Hockley's works on film are informed by his experience as a psycho-therapist as he uses films in his private practice. In his monographs, he explores the affective power of cinema and television. In *Frames of Mind: A Post-Jungian Look at Cinema, Television and Technology* (2007), Hockley rightly notes that academic film theory surprisingly paid little attention to viewers' emotional relationships with the mobbing [CH3] image (Hockley, 2007: 35). In *Somatic Cinema* (2014), he further investigates the relation-ship between affect evoked in an individual in the process of watching a movie, and the meaning arising out of this experience. Hockley argues (in line with Jung's view of symbols) that any meaning produced by on-screen imagery is both powerful and personal.

Similarly, Greg Singh's approach to cinema focuses on the affective nature of film viewing – and particularly on the power that affect has on individuals and personality development. In his book *Feeling Film: Affect and Authenticity in Popular Cinema* (2014), Singh argues that cinema is an ideal candidate 'for thinking through the expressive potential of cultural production from a psychological perspective' because, being 'psychomi-metic', it reflects the relationship human beings have with the outside world (Singh, 2014: 11).

Overall, analytical psychology is a versatile toolbox which has a lot to offer to film criticism well beyond the concept of individuation and the hero myth. It can be used to discuss the semiotic/symbolic division, the dichotomy between the universality of the symbol and the personal meanings it generates, the fleeting nature of meaning and affect, the psy-chological value of the hero myth, the relationship between the social and the personal in cinematic narratives, and the nature of the creative process – be it the process of making a film or the process of watching one.

Screenwriting cookbook: Christopher Vogler

The screenwriter and development executive Christopher Vogler particularly capitalized on the founding concepts of Jungian psychology: the individuation process and archetypes. In his book, *The Hero's Journey: Mythic Structure for Writers* (1998) Vogler transforms the ideas of Joseph Campbell and Carl Jung into a sort of Hollywood cookbook aimed at helping screenwriters create commercial yet spiritually meaningful narratives. *The Hero's Journey* is an interesting phenomenon in the world of writing guides and psychoanalytic criticism. It blatantly defies the prevalence of Freudian thinking in the cinematic arena, both in its style and content, and asserts the usefulness and supremacy of the Jungian approach to screen narratives.

It is not just the structure that Vogler borrows from Jung and Campbell. In the introduction to the book, he is very particular about infusing visual images with meaning and spirituality – he firmly believes that the goldmine, the structure he discovered, is not only commercial, but also capable of making people think and improve their lives. The motivation behind the book was to create a template for personally meaningful stories. His working as a story analyst for Fox 2000 taught him that good films were affecting the organs of his body 'in various ways, and really good ones were stimulation more than one organ' (Vogler, 2007: x). Even his writing style has elements of 'new age' thinking in it:

> A book goes out like a wave rolling over the surface of the sea. Ideas radiate from the author's mind and collide with other minds, triggering new waves that return to the author. These generate further thoughts and emanations, and so it goes. The concepts described in *The Writer's Journey* have radiated and are now echoing back interesting challenges and criticisms as well as sympathetic vibrations. This is my report on the waves that have washed back over me from publication of the book, and on the new waves I send back in response.
>
> (2007: xiii)

Vogler takes different archetypes – the hero, the trickster, the shadow, the mentor (wise old man or woman) etc. – and analyses each of them with examples from (mostly popular Hollywood) films. He also separates the hero's journey into phases or steps (call to adventure, refusal of the call, meeting with the mentor, the ordeal reward, the road back, etc.), and discusses each of them in detail. Curiously, Vogler mixes Jung's and Freud's ideas in an attempt to create his own analytical language; for instance: 'In psychological terms, the archetype of the Hero represents what Freud called the ego – that part of the personality that separates from the mother, that considers itself distinct from the human race' (2007: 29).

Vogler's proposed narrative structure follows that outlined by Campbell in *A Hero with a Thousand Faces* rather faithfully. Underlying Campbell's monomyth (the common pattern found in most narratives all around the world) is the anthropological concept of the rites of passage: separation – initiation – return (Campbell, 1968: 23). The only trait that unites all mono-myth heroes is 'being different' from the rest of their community. In other words, they attract extreme reactions from the people around them. In everything else, they are completely different: they can be very stupid or very intelligent; complete failures or very successful; very handsome or, by contrast, not at all attractive. Yet, the protagonist remains unfulfilled because he or she does not comply with the norms of his community. The composite hero of the monomyth, Campbell argues:

> . . . is a personage of exceptional gifts. Frequently he is honoured by his society, frequently unrecognised or disdained. He and/or the world in which he finds himself suffers from a symbolical deficiency. In fairy tales this may be as slight as the lack of a certain golden ring, whereas in apocalyptic vision the physical and spiritual life of the whole earth can be represented as fallen, or on the point of falling into ruin. [. . .]
>   Whether the hero be ridiculous or sublime, Greek or barbarian, gentile of Jew, his journey varies little in essential plan.
>
> (1968: 29–30)

According to Campbell, narrative is a way of organizing the often confus-ing signals coming from the unconscious. Without structure (and narrative provides a firm structure for often subliminal life experiences), we would drown in impressions, fears, choices and instinctive reactions. Narratives hold together the experience of being human. Echoing Jung, Campbell writes: 'The unconscious sends all sorts of vapours, odd beings, terrors and deluding images up into the mind – whether in dream, broad daylight, or insanity; for the human kingdom, beneath the floor of the comparatively neat little dwelling that we call our consciousness, goes down into unsus-pected Alladin caves' (1968: 5).

Campbell writes about personal mythology via dream-work, but he does not make the obvious connection between cinema and dreams. The result of this omission is that it neglects the collective element of contemporary mythology. It transpires that Campbell insists on the personal and intimate aspects of modern narratives, but seems to forget that radio and cinema had been producing immediately accessible narratives for at least fifty years. Campbell's individual is torn from his roots, and his psychological survival depends on the ability of psychoanalysis to interpret his private dreams. The public, easily accessible forms of dreams – such as films – are not mentioned.

Vogler proceeds to fill in the obvious gap and picks up this connection. The hero's journey embeds both our general life principles and guidelines for Hollywood screenwriters/executives. This means that films become our dreams, aimed at fulfilling our psychological needs and acting as our mirrors without any mediators – no need for psychoanalysis or philosophy. It is possible to manipulate the audience's emotions, Vogler argues in the 'Ordeal' section, by making the hero's path thorny and unpredictable, by making them empathize with the hero throughout his or her numerous ordeals, by giving them the opportunity to experience extreme emotions in the safety of their homes or movie theatre: 'People pay good money for a taste of death. Bungee-jumping, skydiving and terrifying amusement park rides give the jolt that awakens fuller appreciation of life. Adventure films and stories are always popular because they offer a less risky way to experience death and rebirth, through heroes we can identify with' (Vogler, 2007: 160).

Cinema is individuation personified. More so than fiction thanks to its visuality, it has always been a sort of condensed and accelerated individuation process; a sort of commercial version of the hero myth. Jung's writings on contemporary individuation are indispensable for film studies, primarily because most cinematic narratives attempt to define the individual and to provide commentary on his relationship with society. In fact, cinema is a form of mass individuation; a form of self-reflection for large groups of people. Cinema provides a platform for the discussion of cultural, social and political problems.

There is a shadow side to all this and, as a result of Vogler's further commercialization of the individuation structure, cinema and television have become machines generating individuation narratives for busy viewers who are no longer aware of their psychological processes, their place in the environment or ways of connecting with other human beings. This kind of viewer does not have time for musing over things or thinking about 'life, the universe and everything'. In this way, individuation becomes externalized and is presented in a processed form, rather like nicely packaged supermarket products.

Selling with Jung: marketing

Analytical Psychology has been employed by a variety of industries and disciplines, marketing perhaps being the most surprising of them all. Marketing saw in it an opportunity to create 'a system for the management of meaning' that would attract consumers, as the authors of the most influential book on Jungian branding, Margaret Mark and Carol S. Pearson, put it. This is not surprising given the image of Jungian psychology as a discipline preoccupied with the purpose and wholeness of human existence. Why not then turn it into a profitable business, selling meaning-making properties of Jungian psychology to the public?

Mark and Pearson write: 'Today the brand is a repository, not merely of functional characteristics, but of meaning and value. But if we are to identify and effectively leverage the essential elements, or "immutables", of our brands, we must become fluent in the visual and verbal language of archetypes' (Mark and Pearson, 2001: 1). They assert that archetypal meaning is 'the driver of product development' and the product is a mere prop in 'archetypal drama' (2001: 20–4). Brands are 'amongst the most vibrant contemporary expressions of these deep and abiding patterns' (2001: 11). Moreover, this is achieved not by artificially attaching meaning to a car or a lipstick, but by creating a real emotional connection between the product and the customer, whereby the product eventually becomes a brand icon (2001: 11). Customer experience and brand loyalty depend on this connection (2001: 43). Even the postmodern customer, used to the vortex of change, loss of life-organizing rituals, artificial identities and lack of authenticity, still seeks meaning – for having a meaningful existence is a fundamental part of being human.

Mark and Pearson also re-write Jung's original archetypes to fit in with marketing principles and come up with twelve new 'archetypes': Innocent, Explorer, Sage, Hero, Outlaw, Magician, Regular Guy/Gal, Lover, Jester, Caregiver, Creator and Ruler. For instance, the Lover branding archetype reflects the desire 'to attain intimacy and experience sensual pleasure, and is embodied in such brands as Godiva chocolate and Haagen Dazs ice cream' (2001: 178–9). The Caregiver image, which is all about nurturing others and enabling their personal growth, may be portrayed in a canned soup brand, or a bank or building society. The Creator 'archetype' can be represented in a makeup or a hair dye brand as they are focused on inspiration for self-transformation (2001: 212–30). One brand may epitomize two or more 'archetypes', such as the Creator/Jester or the Hero/Outlaw combinations.

Other examples of 'archetypal marketing' include Hartwell and Chen's *Archetypes in Branding: A Toolkit for Creatives and Strategists* (2012) and Peter Schaible's *The Secret Weapon of a Master Direct Response Online Copywriter: How to Position Your Brand for Success, Based on the Research of Swiss Psychiatrist Carl Jung* (2011).

This approach appears to be quite callous. Literature on branding has always insisted that what people actually seek in a product is less practical functionality and more of a sort of prosthetic identity; a replacement of genuine personality traits, emotions and relationships. 'Jungian marketing' goes further: it offers 'consumer individuation', a way of becoming oneself via purchasing particular products. It is about acquiring meaning through consumer capitalism. The assumption behind this approach is that it is possible to solve one's emotional issues and construct one's identity by buying a BMW, a MacBook or Prada bag.

Analytical Psychology promises to help us find our unique way in this maze of lifestyles and meanings. Ultimately, Jungian marketing is reductive. What this approach is exploiting is the individuation instinct, the urge for that very elusive unity of the psyche which Jung called the self. Meaning will always be a valid currency, particularly in the fractured postmodern, post-truth world in which multiple sources of identities and information confuse the individual.

Summary

Analytical Psychology has many applications outside the clinic. Literary and art critics have successfully applied Jungian concepts to narratives and works of art pretty much from the start, and the past twenty years saw the emergence of Jungian film studies and Jungian marketing. To art criticism, narrative analysis and marketing, Jungian theory offers structuring devices (archetypes, individuation), provides tools to analyse the creative process (the collective unconscious, active imagination, dream-work, alchemy) and sociocultural commentary (modern man in search for meaning in the increasingly fragmenting world).

However, it is important to avoid the pitfalls of over-commercialization and reductionism when applying Jungian theory to non-clinical phenomena, as this would turn the analytical process into an exercise of identifying the correct individuation milestones and archetypes in the narrative.

Bibliography

Bassil-Morozow, H. (2010). *Tim Burton: The Monster and the Crowd*. London: Routledge.

Bassil-Morozow, H. (2012). *The Trickster in Contemporary Film*. London: Routledge.

Bassil-Morozow, H. (2015). *Identity and Agency in Contemporary Society*. London and New York: Routledge.

Bordwell, David (2007). *Poetics of Cinema*. London: Routledge.

Campbell, Joseph (1959). *The Masks of Gods: Primitive Mythology*. New York: Viking.

Campbell, Joseph (1968). *The Hero with a Thousand Faces*. Novato, CA: New World Library, 2008.

Dennison, John (2015). *Seamus Heaney and the Adequacy of Poetry*. Oxford: Oxford University Press.

Dickens, Charles (1861). *Great Expectations*. London: Penguin, 2003.

Fordham, Frieda (1966). *An Introduction to Jung*. London: Penguin.

Fredericksen, D. (1979). 'Jung/Sign/Symbol/Film', in I. Alister & C. Hauke (eds.), *Jung and Film: Post-Jungian Takes on the Moving Image* (pp. 17–55). London: Routledge, 2001.

Freud, Sigmund (1910). 'Leonardo da Vinci and a Memory of His Childhood', in J. Strachey (ed. and trans.), *The Standard Edition of the Complete Psychological Works of Sigmund Freud* (Vol. 11; pp. 59–139). London: Vintage, 1960, 2001.

Freud, Sigmund (1914). 'On Narcissism: An Introduction', in J. Strachey (ed. and trans.), *The Standard Edition of the Complete Psychological Works of Sigmund Freud* (Vol. 14; pp. 67–102). London: Vintage, 1960, 2001.

Freud, Sigmund (1920). *Beyond the Pleasure Principle*, in J. Strachey (ed. and trans.), *The Standard Edition of the Complete Psychological Works of Sigmund Freud* (Vol. 18; pp. 7–67). London: Vintage, 1960, 2001.

Freud, Sigmund (1928). 'Dostoevsky and Parricide', in J. Strachey (ed. and trans.), *The Standard Edition of the Complete Psychological Works of Sigmund Freud* (Vol. 21; pp. 177–195). London: Vintage, 1960, 2001.

Hauke, C. (2000). *Jung and the Postmodern: The Interpretation of Realities*. London and Philadelphia: Routledge.

Hauke, C. (2005). *Human Being Human: Culture and the Soul*. London: Routledge.

Hauke, C. (2014). *Visible Mind: Movies, Modernity and the Unconscious*. London: Routledge.

Hauke, C. & Alister, I. (2001). *Jung and Film: Post-Jungian Takes on the Moving Image*. London: Routledge.

Hauke, C. & Hockley, L. (2011). *Jung and Film II: The Return, Further Post-Jungian Takes on the Moving Image*. London and New York: Routledge.

Hockley, L. (2001). *Cinematic Projections: The Analytical Psychology of C. G. Jung and Film Theory*. London: University of Luton Press.

Hockley, L. (2007). *Frames of Mind: A Post-Jungian Look at Cinema, Television and Technology*. Bristol and Chicago: Intellect.

Hockley, L. (2014). *Somatic Cinema*. London: Routledge.

Izod, J. (2001). *Myth, Mind and Screen: Understanding the Heroes of Our Time*. London: Routledge.

Izod, J. (2006). *Screen, Culture, Psyche: A Post-Jungian Approach to Working with the Audience*. London: Routledge.

Jacobi, Jolande (1942). *The Psychology of C. G. Jung* (eighth edition), trans. Ralph Manheim. New Haven and London: Yale University Press, 1973.

Jacobi, Jolande (ed.) (1953). *Psychological Reflections: An Anthology of the Writings of C. G. Jung*. London: Routledge and Kegan Paul.

Jacobi, Jolande (1964). 'Symbols in an Individual Analysis', in C. G. Jung and Marie-Louise von Frantz (eds.), *Man and His Symbols* (pp. 323–374). London: Picador.

Jacoby, Mario (1994). *Shame and the Origins of Self-Esteem*. London: Routledge, 1996.

Jacoby, Mario (2009). *The Cultural Turn: Selected Writings on the Postmodern, 1983–1998*. London: Routledge.

Jacoby, Mario (2010). *Individuation and Narcissism*. Hove: Routledge.

Jung C. G. (1962). *Memories, Dreams, Reflections*. London: Fontana, 1995.

Jung C. G. (1970–1979). *The Collected Works* (CW), ed. Herbert Read, Michael Fordham & Gerhardt Adler, trans. R. F. C. Hull. London: Routledge.

Jung, C. G. & von Franz, Marie-Louise (eds.) (1964). *Man and His Symbols*. London: Picador, 1978.

Kerényi, Karl (1956). 'The Trickster in Relation to Greek Mythology', in Paul Radin (ed.), *The Trickster: A Study in American Indian Mythology*. New York: Schocken Books.

Klein, M. (1975a). *Envy and Gratitude*. London: Vintage, 1997.

Klein, M. (1975b). *The Psycho-Analysis of Children*. London: Vintage, 1997.

Klein, M. (1975c). *Love, Guilt and Reparation*. London: Vintage, 1988.

Mark, Margaret and Pearson, Carol S. (2001). *The Hero and the Outlaw: Building Extraordinary Brands through the Power of Archetypes*. New York: McGraw-Hill.

Murdock, Maureen (1990). *The Heroine's Journey: A Woman's Quest for Wholeness*. Boston, MA: Shambhala.

Neumann, Erich (1959). *Art and the Creative Unconscious: Four Essays*. Princeton: Princeton University Press, 1974.

Rowland, Susan (2005). *Jung as a Writer*. London: Routledge.

Samuels, Andrew (1985). *Jung and the Post-Jungians*. London: Routledge.

Samuels, Andrew (2015). *Passions, Persons, Psychotherapy, Politics: The Selected Works of Andrew Samuels*. London: Routledge.

Singh, G. (2009). *Film after Jung: Post-Jungian Approaches to Film Theory*. London: Routledge.

Singh, G. (2014). *Feeling Film: Affect and Authenticity in Popular Cinema*. Hove: Routledge.

Swales, John (1993) *Genre Analysis: English in Academic and Research Settings*, Cambridge: Cambridge University Press.

Vogler, C. (1998). *The Writer's Journey: Mythic Structure for Writers* (revised edition). London: Pan.

Von Frantz, Marie-Louise (1964). 'The Process of Individuation', in C. G. Jung & Marie-Louise von Frantz (eds.), *Man and His Symbols* (pp. 159–254). London: Picador.

Von Frantz, Marie-Louise (1970). *An Introduction to the Interpretation of Fairytales*. Zurich: Spring Publications, 1973.

Waddell, T. (2006). *Mis/takes: Archetype, Myth and Identity in Screen Fiction*. London and New York: Routledge.

Waddell, T. (2009). *Wild/lives: Trickster, Place and Liminality on Screen*. London: Routledge.

Index

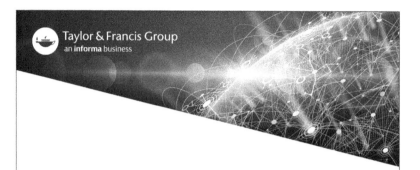

Milton Keynes UK
Ingram Content Group UK Ltd.
UKHW022139051023
430040UK00009B/101